ep sport

Judo

CW00894807

ep sport

Judo

Geof Gleeson

A&C Black · London

First published 1988 by
A & C Black (Publishers) Limited
35 Bedford Row, London WC1R 4JH

© 1988 Geof Gleeson

ISBN 0 7136 5589 5

British Library Cataloguing in
Publication Data
Gleeson, G. R.
    Judo.———(EP sport).
    1. Judo
    I. Title
    796.8'152   GV1114

    ISBN 0—7136—5589—5

Typeset by the Pindar Group of
Companies, Scarborough, North Yorkshire.

Printed and bound in Great Britain by
R. J. Acford, Chichester.

CONTENTS

Foreword   6

INTRODUCTION   7

1   THE START   8
Skills needed to win a judo
   contest   10
How do you start a
   contest?   11
How to score yuko (5) and koka
   (3)   14
Ground wrestling or
   grappling   18
Break-outs   21
What does the novice need to
   know about grips?   23
Some more small score
   attacks   24
Two brief lesson outlines   28

2   THE MIDDLE   30
Movement training   31
Strangles and arm locks   32
Ipponseoinage   37
Avoiding and countering   39
Uchimata and haraigoshi   40
Sutemiwaza/body throws   42
Ashiwaza/foot trips   49
Hands-only throws   50
No-hands throws   51
What are tactics and how can
   they be created?   54
Some tactical building
   bricks   59
Thinking   62
A typical lesson plan   65

3   THE END   67
Some attitudes to the end
   game   67
About winning and losing   69
Examples of tired skills   71
What about tactics?   73
Kata   81
Randori (freeplay)   86
Shiai (competition)   86
Skill acquisition   86
Motivation   87
Summary   89
More linked attacks:
counters   90

INDEX   96

Acknowledgements

First, I must thank Messrs Andrew Cheshire, Simon Hill, Keith Cannaby and Peter Barnett for their help. Keith has many times been British Champion and has helped before with the illustrations of my books. His ability to produce top level skills in national championships and to act as the 'Mr White' in this book (and others) is a very rare talent indeed. I am most appreciative of the time he has given me. Mr Barnett not only trained Keith but is *primus inter pares* in relation to the best coaches in the U.K. His help and knowledge over the past many years have always been unstinted. I am most grateful for that and for his friendship. I should like to add a special thank you to Mrs Pat Cropper M.B.E. for allowing us to use the Norman Green Athletic Centre.

My thanks go to the British Judo Association for allowing me to print the various extrapolations from its contest rules.

Finally, a family thank you: to my son Finn for taking all the photographs—with patience and tolerance; to my long suffering wife who with no complaint typed yet another judo book. What can a writer do for such a wife but to say a humble thank you? (She insists Sula, our daughter, kept her sane with her ready laughter!)

FOREWORD

Geof Gleeson, formerly the chief national coach for the British Judo Association and presently executive-secretary for the British Association of National Coaches, has been involved in coaching for over 30 years. Geof has developed his own particular style, both as a man and as a coach. He has never been afraid to expose himself to new ideas or to express his opinions openly. To quote from the text of the book ... 'Whenever I had something to say I have said it in the manner in which I have felt it ought to be said' (Picasso).

My advice to you, the reader, is to go no further unless you are ready to be challenged and are willing to reassess your own viewpoint. Geof would be the first to encourage you to debate, discuss or disagree with his ideas. Coaching, like performance, is a very personal matter and each individual will undoubtedly develop differently. Throughout the text Geof repeats the need for flexibility and for each coach to understand basic principles. It is these basic principles with which the National Coaching Foundation are concerned. We believe that by allowing every coach access to a range of educational opportunities we will encourage them to understand more about the human body and mind. The 'thinking' coach who emerges should be inquisitive, innovative and, above all, flexible.

Geof gives us an insight into the physical, mental and spiritual requirements of judo players at all levels. He constantly reminds us that theory and practice are closely intertwined and that the coach learns to apply principles to performance through experience and practice.

As well as being a most interesting and thorough guide to judo, the book is also worthy of finding its way on to the bookshelf of anyone concerned with the art of coaching.

Sue Campbell
Director,
National Coaching
Foundation

INTRODUCTION

Judo has been the subject of much interest outside Japan during the past 30 years or so. It has joined the hallowed ranks of Olympic sports; millions practise it and there have been innumerable books written about it. Yet it still remains a shadowy activity; it still gets classified generally with Japanese martial arts and even the judo establishment does not seem to have made up its mind whether it is supporting a system of self defence or a Japanese feudal fighting method.

This slow appreciation of, what is to me, a great complexity of intricate and finely balanced skills caused me enormous frustration when I was a young man. I could not understand why people who had generously dedicated themselves to the development of judo could then only see it as a very narrow, even clumsy performance of simple body mechanics instead of viewing judo as a wide range of skills demanding a great depth of knowledge and inspiration. They insisted on seeing it as some kind of mindless, ritual performance. All that was needed, apparently, was to repeat several times a few movements abstracted from the total skill and that would enable them to acquire the ability to perform all the skills!

That was in my youth. Now I no longer worry about such matters. If people want to undervalue judo, it is of no concern to me. However, I must admit I do still feel an odd twitch of frustration when I see novices being taught so little about the intricacies and beauty of judo.

In this book I write about judo as a sport; not the kind of sport that says winning is the only thing worth doing, but the sort of sport the Greeks of the fifth century B.C. would have understood as a mix of philosophy and physical culture. Socrates warned against neglecting the body, but at the same time he also opposed the excesses of athletic training.

In taking this approach I shall base the book upon competition, i.e. upon the contest in which one person matches himself against another within accepted rules. The text, therefore, like the contest, will be divided into the beginning, the middle and the end. A contest is, of course, only a microcosm of the whole training programme. So, discussions about the competition will also contain references to points on the training programme, such as when do you start a contest and when, indeed, is it ended? Is there always a phase between these two arbitrary limits?

I hope you will find this presentation useful and interesting and that you enjoy both the reading and the doing.

Geof Gleeson

1 THE START

The two black belts stand 4 metres apart from each other in the middle of an island of space measuring 10 metres × 10 metres. Hundreds of people stare down at them from rows of seats that go right to the back of the stadium. The atmosphere is electric; the evening is set for drama. The two men look at each other as if neither exists. The referee, standing in the same island, shouts 'Hajime!' and both men jerk imperceptibly into life. They bow and move forwards. They have approximately five minutes in front of them to prove that their years of training have not been wasted and they have learned their jobs like true professionals.

Let's follow them through the contest, face the many decisions they have to face and see what kind of training they should have had (and will have to have if their performance is to be successful in the future).

The one intention that underlies all tactical thoughts that are now racing round in their heads is to win! How does one win, or lose, in a judo match? The rules give the answers, so let's look at them and see what they say. Every fighter must know them.

A match is won by various means, consisting of ippon, wazaari, yuko, koka. They are:

Ippon (*Article 21*)

The referee shall announce 'ippon' when in his opinion an applied technique corresponds with the following criteria:

(a) A contestant, with control, throws the other contestant largely on the back with considerable force and speed.

(b) A contestant holds, with osaekomi, the other contestant, who is unable to get away for 30 seconds after the announcement of osaekomi.

(c) A contestant gives up by tapping twice or more with his hand or foot, or says 'maita' (give up), generally as a result of a grappling technique, shime-waza (strangle) or kansetsu-waza (arm-lock).

(d) The effect of a strangle technique or arm lock is sufficiently apparent.

Waza-Ari (*Article 24*)

The referee shall announce 'waza-ari' when in his opinion the applied technique corresponds with the following criteria:

(a) A contestant, with control, throws the other contestant, but the technique is partially lacking in one of the three elements necessary for ippon (see Article 21a and rules Appendix).

(b) A contestant holds, with osaekomi, the other contestant who is unable to get away for 25 seconds or more, but less than 30 seconds.

Yuko (*Article 26*)

The referee shall announce 'yuko' when in his opinion the applied technique corresponds with the following criteria:

(a) A contestant, with control, throws the other contestant, but the technique is partially lacking in two

of the three elements necessary for ippon.

e.g. (i) Partially lacking in the element of 'largely on the back' and also in one of the other two elements of 'speed' or 'force'.

(ii) Largely on the back, but partially lacking in both the other two elements of 'speed' and 'force' (see Appendix, 'Side of body').

(b) A contestant holds, with osaekomi, the other contestant who is unable to get away for 20 seconds or more, but less than 25 seconds.

Koka (*Article 26*)

The referee shall announce 'koka' when in his opinion the applied technique corresponds with the following criteria:

(a) A contestant throws the other contestant onto his thigh(s) or buttocks with speed and force.

(b) A contestant holds, with osaekomi, the other contestant who is unable to get away for 10 seconds or more, but less than 20 seconds.

Osaekomi (*Article 27*)

The referee shall announce 'osaekomi' when in his opinion the applied technique corresponds with the following criteria:

(a) The contestant being held is controlled by his opponent and has his back, both shoulders or one shoulder in contact with the mat.

(b) The control is made from the side, from the rear or from on top.

(c) The contestant applying the hold does not have his leg(s) controlled by his opponent's leg(s).

Several points will strike the uninitiated straight away. First, all the terms are in Japanese; this is in deference to judo's origin, but it does not help the novice or the spectator to comprehend what is happening. That is a fault! For the novice performer, however, it is no great restriction, since he can learn the terms fast enough. As for the spectators, they have to put up with it and do the best they can!

The next point to notice is how vague the demarcation is between the scores; the identification is left almost entirely to the discretion of the referee (another fault). It does mean, of course, that the performer has to study these differences so that he knows better what is happening, both when he makes a score and when he loses it. These scoring values must be built into his tactical playing of the match.

In many ways it is remarkable how little judo competition has changed since its inception about a hundred years ago. Participants still wear the same style of kit as the fighters did over a century ago, in spite of its inadequacy in satisfying contemporary needs (e.g. body heat control, audience recognition) and in particular its inability to fulfil technical requirements (see later). Similarly, the skills have evolved very little, due mainly to the stultifying effects of the rules. The rules demand a 'death-or-glory' approach—get one full ippon and the scorer has won there and then. Such an approach may appear to some to have certain advantages, as for example it did to the Japanese Army—which invented the system before the Second World War as a way of training suicide pilots. However, for a sporting event it is completely inappropriate. Not only does it discourage any development of tactical skills, but it makes spectating very boring. Imagine what would happen if a football match were terminated after the first goal was scored!

This potential tedium was recognised reluctantly by the 'powers-that-be' and so about 20 years ago they introduced some minor scores, yuko and koka, in an attempt to stimulate interest for the spectator. It was not successful because the referee had now to distinguish three lines of demarcation instead of one and all were equally obscure! Perhaps some day those same powers-that-be will bring the competitive rules of judo up-to-date.

SKILLS NEEDED TO WIN A JUDO CONTEST

Before trying to provide answers it would be helpful if 'skills' were defined, if only in relation to judo. 'Skill' is one of those culture words, like art, that everyone uses with great familiarity but with very little idea of what it means. It is, of course, difficult to define and to arrive at one short definition to encompass all its meanings is extremely difficult. However, if several definitions are made, relating to the various aspects of skill, perhaps some composite picture of what it actually means can be built up. Here two are offered, each one with its own particular advantage and disadvantage. The first is the well-known statement from Barbara Knapp (*Skill in Sport*, 1963):

> Skill is the learned ability to bring about predetermined results with maximum certainty, often with the minimum outlay of time or energy or both.

The other is the author's:

> Skill is the trained spontaneity to exploit an ephemeral set of circumstances, in order to achieve a predetermined conclusion.

If we mix these two disparate definitions and then extrapolate some common elements it may give us an indication of the kind of characteristics the individual needs to acquire those skills. First, there must be an innate, natural ability to do and know the essentialities of the skill: for example, for some skills (like judo) participants must be able to locate their body in space, at any instant; they must be able to feel situations through their bodies and know how to respond to them (allowing the body to think for itself, see chapter 3); they must be able to think comprehensively and about the total situation, not just about parts of it (see chapter 2).

These skills and many more will be demanded. The champion will possess a number of them, but not all, and that is why he has to train so hard—to fill those innate gaps in his own particular 'tool kit'. The top performer must know how to learn by insight, not rote, when he needs to use force or cunning. He will need to appreciate aesthetic qualities, how to exploit them for his own ends and how to plan the use of rhythms and movement patterns to accomplish what he has to do. Lastly, he must be able to keep rules and appreciate how they underpin a moral code of behaviour which must be upheld if sport is to be a legitimate part of society.

No doubt the reader will be thinking about those hoary old conundrums, 'Are champions born or made?' and 'Is it nature or nurture?' For me there is little doubt: champions must be born. They must have those essentialities of a skill—like hand and eye co-ordination for a ball-game player—before they start training. After that, of course, they must have the help of the environment. If they are born swimmers, they must take the precaution of being born where there is water! They must have parents who indulge their search for performance; they need to find a coach who lives the skills and can empathise with their search for adequacy; and, lastly, they must find competitors who compete with honour.

The searching athlete, with his coach and the right training environment, can start about the business of learning the many aspects that go to make up the total skill of top performance. Between them they can develop those innate qualities into a talent that will take the individual as far as he wants to go, the complexity of which will amaze the rest of the sport's fraternity. Polished talent plus transcendental skills make for an inspired performance.

Specific techniques must be studied and learned, but they are not as important as a number of judo coaches believe. No doubt some of the confusion between technique and skill can be traced back to the Japanese word 'waza'. 'Waza' can mean technique, skill, trick, performance, art, work; the

Japanese cannot differentiate between these meanings. English is a very rich language. The purpose of the training programme is to discover how these techniques can be modified to suit different sorts of circumstances within a judo contest, so that a successful result can be achieved. That is the most important point. Some coaches claim there must be set objectives within a training programme in order to monitor progress. For some sports that may well be true, but for an 'open' sport like judo objectives can become as much a barrier to growth as a stimulus for improvement. The fighter must learn to analyse situations so that he can adapt and modify his plans to overcome the wiles of the opponent. Fixed objectives can limit and even smother that process. Flexibility is the key word.

Finally, there are the strategic skills, which need to be learned; for example, when are new skills to be added to the repertoire in order to beat a newly developed fashion of fighting? when should an individual train for more power and when for stamina? when should a new kata be structured for some specific skill improvement? After this, how do these strategies feed back and influence the single tactical skill of fighting a total contest?

A contest is full of paradox and opposites. The fighter must be fast and spontaneous if he wishes to attack successfully, yet he must also move very slowly with complete control over his actions. He must be able to generate a great deal of power if he is to impose his tactical plan on the opponent, but he must be very 'soft' and sensitive if he is to distinguish the subtle and minute movements the opponent will make in preparation for launching an attack. The final outcome of the contest will depend largely on the relationship between the two fighters. This relationship continually changes, both in physical terms, e.g. in terms of the spaces around and between them, and in psychological terms, e.g. who has the strongest personality and when? How does each fighter cope with these changing relationships? During the rest of the book several of the ways some fighters deal with this will be looked at.

HOW DO YOU START A CONTEST?

Carefully! If the opponent has been fought before or has been watched critically over any period, a tactical plan should already have been generated. If the opponent is a complete stranger, a plan will be devised as the match progresses, utilising small, segmental, tactical 'parts' experienced in previous matches and in training.

The opponent's movement patterns and rhythms must be quickly assessed. Does he move smoothly or erratically? Does he jerk from one direction to another, or does he glide? Is he a left or a right attacker? As a guide, if he steps forward at the match start with his left foot, he is a left thrower, whereas if he steps forward with his right foot, he is a right thrower. An experienced fighter will usually try to hide this habit as long as he can. Smooth movers tend to throw forwards, and jerky movers, backwards. To help find out more, low score attacks (3 or 5) are used. (Some outward going personalities do go straight for the high scores of 7 or 10, but there are few of these in the judo fraternity.) Such attacks will have little body weight commitment and therefore will be 'safe' (from counter-attack) and perhaps, if done with confidence, they may even make a score!

Much can be learned from how the opposition responds to these small attacks. Such information will be instantly fed into the tactical planning 'computer' brain. If the opponent reacts very quickly all attacks must be done fast, carefully *and accurately*, for he will be a good counter man. If he reacts slowly, attacks need to be powerful and slow. The message here, of course, is that different sorts of throws are used for different situations. In terms of learning that can be summed up by the two following statements:

1. If different throws are used for different circumstances, e.g. ipponseoinage is used for the slow and powerful circumstance and uchimata for the fast and careful one, the technique will not ideally vary much, but

2. if the same preferred throw is used in all circumstances, then it must be greatly or slightly modified to suit the different and varied conditions experienced: e.g. if taiotoshi is used on every occasion, then the use of body weight and leg position will have to be changed considerably to exploit each particular circumstance.

There is one last point to consider before we start trying out specific ideas. The whole battle plan is dominated by what an army general would call 'the lie of the land'; in a judo context this means when and where is the best place, within the contest area, to achieve a particular effect and how are the spaces around both fighters to be controlled? How the spaces are controlled will depend on where the fighters are in the contest area (see page 14). There are guide-lines for understanding what these spaces are and how they can be used (see photographs 1(a)—(d)).

1 **Fighting spaces** Who is to control the gap?
(a) White wants the starting space to be large ...

(b) so he can turn completely in that space.

(c) The space is closed to ensure maximum transfer of power. Black goes up and over.

(d) The space is opened up again so Black can be 'steered' into the ground.

In simple terms they are:

1. When the two fighters first make contact, they automatically create space between them. Initially it is neutral, but the struggle to control it begins immediately. Who can manipulate the size of the intervening space for his own advantage?

2. When a fighter thinks he has gained control of the spaces, he will be able to attack. It becomes his 'attacking space', meaning that he has to create as large a space as possible, between the two bodies, in which he can develop adequate momentum and power to overcome the opponent's defences.

3. Having done that and moved towards the opponent—the attacking movement—he must now create the 'throwing space', which must be as small as necessary to transmit sufficient power to the opponent in the form of whatever attacking technique has been selected.

4. The relationship of attacking and throwing spaces will indicate clearly the score intended and therefore the difference between throwing and landing directions selected (see photographs 2(a)—(c)).

Throwing and landing directions

This throw has the same name as that in the photograph sequence 1(a)–(d), i.e. taiotoshi. It can be used to throw the opponent forwards, as in photograph sequence 1, or backwards, as in 2.

2 (a) The start is the same as that in photograph 1(a).

(b) Since a big turn is not necessary, the attacking space is kept small. This minimises countering opportunities. Black is driven backwards, which minimises falling space and makes turn-outs difficult.

(c) Black does not have to fall over White's body. The drop is short and the score is small. It is a 'safe' attack, but it is an extremely effective one.

If there is little difference between attacking and throwing space (the attacking space being only slightly larger than the throwing space), the score will usually be small; if the difference is big (the attacking space being much larger than the throwing space), the scores will be big, i.e. 7 or 10. (See photographs 1(a)—(d).) Similarly, if the 'landing direction' (i.e. the line in which the opponent falls) is roughly the same as the 'throwing direction' (i.e. the direction in which the opponent was thrown, at the point of kake, see page 18), the score will be small; if the throwing direction is much different from the landing direction, the score will be big. Look at photograph 1 again, because the right foot of the opponent is back (see 1a). The direction of throw is somewhat sideways, but the man falls forwards – a big score. In photograph 2 the throw is backward and he falls backwards – a small score.

5. The location of the attack within the contest area will decide, to some extent, the type of attack used, and therefore the size and the relationship of the spaces created, and then finally the degree of score made. For example, if an attack is made on the edge of the fighting area, the score will tend to be small because of the restriction of throwing direction caused by the edge itself. The attack in the middle of the contest area will usually result in big scores, because of the unlimited range of throwing directions available.

6. When these various spaces are looked at from the standpoint of the defender, they change their value entirely. For example, when an attack is initiated, the defender must make the space between the bodies as *small* as possible, so limiting the movement of the attacker (the opponent's attacking space). If, in spite of that, the attacker gets through the 'defensive space' and reaches the point where he begins to create a small throwing space, the defender must make that as *big* as possible, which allows him to dissipate the attacker's force and avoid a score. This is the defender's 'avoiding space'.

During the contest the roles of attacker and defender will be changing constantly, every few seconds. The competitors will be trying to change the spaces between them as fast as their roles change. It is this constant change of role, this constant battle of who can control the space, that makes a judo match very exciting for the fighter, but dull for the spectator. The movements can be quite subtle and easily felt by the competitor, but they are difficult for the spectator to see, so he imagines there is little going on and so thinks it is extremely tedious.

Back to the Contest

The referee has called 'Hajime!' The competitors move towards each other, very cautiously. Each man reaches out for the other and wants his leading hand (one hand always leads) to hold first, because it will instantly control space. The other hand blocks the opponent's hold for as long as possible. After a considerable amount of manoeuvring, the other hand grabs hold. As one man grabs cloth, so does the other. They crouch and move sideways, but neither moves forwards (it is too dangerous— sideways is better).

They begin the business of finding out what strengths and weaknesses each has got (see page 30).

How do the competitors attack— by threatening to move in a certain way, or by making small score attacks? Let's see how small scores can be tried.

HOW TO SCORE YUKO (5) AND KOKA (3)

There are two styles of training for low scores, each at the end of a spectrum of purpose dictated by the competitor's level of experience.

1. For the 'black belt' (black belt is being used here to mean a person who has one or two years' solid training and experience): the

man knows that in this particular contest he may be inferior to the opponent (in another contest he may very well be superior). To fight for 10 (ippon) not only will be a waste of time, but may well court early disaster. He therefore trains for 5 or 3 so that he has got a much better chance of successfully scoring something.

2. For the novice: he needs to gain experience in throwing and scoring, but without having to fall down heavily. Small score skills are very useful for him to have.

Somewhere in the centre of the spectrum of low score-training is an area in which the experienced can learn from the novice, and vice versa. The two can train together, the good performer practising his low scoring skills without damaging the novice, while the novice can learn much from the dynamic action of the 'black belt'.

When learning simple throwing or grappling skills, there are two general elements that have to be isolated: the technique and the situation in which it has to be executed. In traditional judo teaching it has always been assumed that the best way is to teach technique first and then to let the performer find his own salvation as far as discovering how the situation modifies the action. The opposite way, to teach situation first and technique second,

has many virtues and, indeed, it will largely be used throughout this book.

Simple Learning Situations (for the novice)

Competitive skills have to be performed in moving and varying circumstances, so they must be learned in moving circumstances. In very simple situations the opponent

3 An easy introduction to throwing and falling
(a) White walks Black backwards.

(c) Black steps over the blocking leg with his right leg, pivots on the right foot . . .

will be assumed to be moving forwards, backwards or sideways.

In all photographs in this book the man in white is the initiator of the attack (he may not always finish it!) The man in black is the reactor who responds to the attack (he may not always lose!)

Black Moving Backwards
Look at photographs 3(a)—(d).

(b) White steps forwards with his right leg, making a block over which he will push Black.

(d) sits down and rolls over easily with no bumps.

Black is moving backwards; White follows, skips forwards and pushes his partner over his extended right leg. Black steps over the right leg, sits and rolls down. (It needs to be done several times.)

Points to notice The throw can be called taiotoshi. One body is approximately at *right angles* to the other. The legs are wide astride and both are comfortably straight. White's left hand is pulling and his right hand is pushing. Space between White and Black is maintained fairly consistently throughout. Score will be 3 or 5.

The step, quarter turn, pull and push happen roughly at the same time.

Check Points
In the business of learning a term 'feed back' is used; it is an almost automatic process in which a purposeful movement is made, the error in achievement is immediately noted and fed back into the mental system, adjustments are made, the movement is corrected and the initial movement (now improved) is repeated. (Some call this 'trial and error'.) The process is repeated until the required degree of accuracy is achieved. So, check the following with throwing practice.

1. *Black* is thrown *sideways* and not forwards, meaning that White does *not* make a half turn (as a terminal score might demand), only a quarter turn. It is a quick and simple movement.

2. White's body is kept upright throughout the movement; he must not 'fall backwards' out of control.

3. By pulling and pushing with each hand White should be able to keep the space between the two bodies roughly constant.

4. White can keep the speed of attack comparatively slow.

5. At the novice's level Black should step over White's extended right leg quickly and easily, sit down and roll over. Look at photographs 3(a)—(d) again.

6. At a black belt level, the stabbing action of the right leg needs to be *very* fast and the pull and push of the hands should also be very hard and fast.

A variation This same attacking movement by White can be done when Black is moving forwards. However, the space between the bodies will be closing thoughout White's quarter turn attack, making it very difficult to complete.

If Black is moving to his *left* side, it will be easy for him to pull White *backwards* when he makes the quarter turn (see photograph 4). When Black is moving to his *right* side, it will make White's quarter turn more effective. Therefore, the best attacking opportunities are when Black is moving backwards or towards his right side. This will be true for both novice and black belt,

4 Slack body-control
White has allowed his weight to drop back onto his heels and his hips to move forwards. Black can easily pull him backwards.

irrespective of the general speed and context of the movement.

Black Moving Forwards
White moves back with Black, then after several steps he makes a small jump onto his left foot and hooks the right leg in behind Black's left leg (see photographs 5(a) and (b)). Black steps back, sits and rolls backwards.

Points to notice The throw can be called ouchigake (or gari). Again,

5 Ouchigake/gari

(a) *Notice Black's right foot is well back, exposing the left leg and making it vulnerable.*

the bodies are at right angles and White is looking towards Black's right side. White quickly lifts Black's left leg with his right leg and then just as quickly puts it to the ground and puts weight on it (so becoming very stable). White's left hand is pulling while his right hand is pushing (as in taiotoshi). Space between the bodies is large. The score is small, 3 or 5.

As before, all actions are to be done at the same time, or as near

(b) *White moves his left foot and then drives his right leg in behind black's left leg. Black lifts his left leg, steps back with it, sits and rolls backwards. Notice how White pulls Black's head well down for control.* **This is very important.**

to that as possible. They should be repeated as often as necessary.

Check points White should jump his left foot 'outside' Black's left foot (see fig. 1). White drives/throws Black over the outside edge of his right foot. White's body shape must be kept strong. If necessary a couple of hops can be used to reinforce the

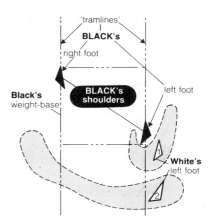

Fig. 1 Optimum positions for 'back' and 'front' throws
White's number 1 left foot: the approximate position for ouchi. The shaded area (1) shows where White can be in order to throw Black forwards/sideways. The shaded area (2) represents where White's left foot can be in order to throw Black backwards/sideways.

driving action of White's hands. For black belts the hooking right leg may not always hook high (into Black's left knee), but it can sweep wide and then stay on the ground (again, stability is most important). (See photographs 5(a) and (b).) Remember, only a score of 3 or 5 is being attempted.

Black's 'falling' action will be much the same in both these throwing actions. Indeed, much of the movement is very similar, so take

17

particular notice of the differences:

1. In taiotoshi Black's right foot is blocked to stop it moving and he is then pushed/turned over it.

2. In ouchigake Black's left leg is raised, so that all his weight is on his right foot and he is then turned over it.

These are two different ways to achieve the same result.

Now that White has a certain feeling of doing these two throws let him try them in free movement. Black and White move around the mat quite easily and smoothly. Black must attempt to emphasise the backward and forward movements with minimal sideways movement to elicit attacks from White. White must try to 'slot' his two attacks into the movement patterns offered by Black. It must be remembered that this kind of training is much more a matter of co-operation—helping each other —than competition (the purpose of competition is to frustrate every developing situation). In a training session for competition there are, of course, no Mr Blacks; all are Mr Whites. Both are changing the roles of attacker and defender as often as is needed.

Other Considerations

If a learner, no matter what his experience, needs to stand still in order to get a clear idea of the basic movement required, that's fine. Stillness does have a place in the learning process. However, he should not spend too much time standing still. Skill is about coping with many movement variables. The ingredients of a skill must be learned in a varying set of circumstances.

The moment of actual throwing (the Japanese term is kake) is the most dangerous for both competitors: for Black, because he is about to fall down and is in danger of losing a terminal score; for White, because he has committed all or most of his effort into the attack, so providing a countering opportunity for Black. Therefore, at that moment both must be very aware of everything that is going on. What is more, they must be prepared to make an instantaneous decision as to what they must do: Black must decide if he is going to twist out of the fall and avoid the terminal score; if Black counters, White must decide what he will do to counter it! The only time a fighter should stop fighting is when the referee tells him to stop.

GROUND WRESTLING OR GRAPPLING

At the beginning of this chapter ways of winning a contest were outlined. One way is by 'osaekomi'. The purpose of this technique is to pin or hold a man on his back for a specified period of time. That sounds easy enough but, like so many things, it quickly becomes difficult. Pinning Black is hard enough when he is obligingly lying still and allowing White to hold him, but when he is trying to avoid being pinned the job becomes virtually impossible. However, it must be done, so get him on his back first and then keep him there!

In the contest which began this chapter it was suggested that the competition would start cautiously. The competitors would try only for small scores, 3 or 5, a fast attack with taiotoshi or ouchigake, and nothing else. That's fine, but what if the man who made such a small score is a ground work specialist? He may well want to try to add to that score an attack on the ground (a sogo score). How would he set about it? First, the opponent may well have gone straight into a defensive crouch as he fell, see photograph 6(a). Now the attacker has to turn him over onto his back. One way of doing it is by using the forearm lever. See in photograph 6(c) how the man facedown is having his left arm used as a lever to turn him over. As he begins to move, the attacker moves quickly into the space (photograph 6(c)) and flattens him out by lying across his chest (photograph 6(d)). Immediately, the position is adjusted, so that a very tight pin is achieved (see photograph 6(d)).

6 A simple turn-over
(a) Black is defending. With his left hand White pulls
    Black forwards 'off balance'.

(b) White begins to put his right arm in, under Black's
    left arm.

(c) Using Black's arm as a lever, and his right leg as a
    power supply, White begins to turn Black over.

(d) White moves into the space that is opened up, and
    so ends up across Black, applying a side-body pin.
    Note that White's legs are wide apart and are
    pushing.

Power Points for Pins

Ground wrestling skills, like throwing skills, are a matter of making the most of what you are given. If you are lucky, you may well find there is everything available that you need: you silently cheer, grab it all and win. At other times there may be very little on offer, so you grab that, too, and hope it is enough.

If a pin (osaekomi) is being tried for, the following ploys are useful to have in mind. Without some of them, it would be a waste of time trying! The first three are necessary for a terminal score; if they cannot be executed, make do with numbers 4 and 5:

1. Control the head; hold it so that it cannot be moved.

2. Have control of one arm (and the shoulder to which it is attached); hold it tight so that it, too, cannot be freed.

3. Be able to 'screw' the head and shoulders tightly together.

4. Have control of one or both hips.

5. Limit the movement of the opponent's legs.

So, back to the pin in the training. Immediately the opponent is turned over, options 1, 2 and 3 above become available. Look at photograph 7 to see how this is done. The whole body of the attacker is 'screwed' into the head and shoulders of the opponent. When done correctly it will be very uncomfortable for the man underneath. When attempts are made to break out of this pin the 'screw' must be made tighter still.

Points to Check

The pin is called kuzurekami shihogatame. The pinning pressure goes through the head into the mat. The attacker's legs should be kept mobile so they can easily follow the movement of the opponent and cancel out any move towards freedom.

What about the novice? As always, technique does not vary between novice and black belt; only the skill varies! Both use the same method of applying force to the opposition; it is only the 'when' and the 'how', i.e. the skill factor, that is different.

In ground wrestling a major skill factor is anticipation. The black belt plans for two or three moves ahead and thereby 'knows' what is going to happen and moves accordingly. He fights in the future. The novice can only fight in the present, but here, too, he must build up experience on movement patterns, not on static poses.

For practice Black gets down on his elbows and knees. Imagine he has just been knocked down for a score of 3 or 5. Knowing how to use the short arm lever is a very useful technique and comes in handy for many situations, so it must be practised often. Go through photographs 6(a)—(d) and make sure every stage is right before moving on to the next one.

Check points Momentum is a very important factor in ground wrestling. It can be used to get the

*7 **Kuzure kamishihogatame***
Note how White keeps his head up so that weight is pressed down on Black. White also tries to entrap Black's arms.

opposition out of static defensive positions like the one illustrated. An attacker generates momentum by moving very quickly in a brief period of time, combining it with his own strength to apply it to the opposition in the most advantageous way. It does have its faults, however; once generated, it is not always easy to check and control.

So, in the turn-over technique, White hooks his right arm in, generates some momentum by moving fast to the side and pushes, turning Black over. However, if care were not taken, Black would keep going and would roll right over onto his front!

White loses the pin. It will happen more easily still if Black intentionally increases his turning rate. This is another of those 'tricks' that can be used in many circumstances in ground wrestling: the attacker generates momentum to overcome a defensive position, succeeds, but then the defender exploits that momentum by causing the attacker to 'over-shoot' and so make himself vulnerable for a counter-attack. Needless to say, the same 'trick' is frequently used in throwing skills.

So, when White turns Black over he must watch for this possibility. He should keep his weight back, not allowing it to move with the turn. Having achieved some facility with

the turn over and pin, White must practise it as often on the other side. He must get used to using Black's right arm as the lever and to pinning from Black's left side.

BREAK-OUTS

In ground wrestling it is obvious that Black has got to break out or escape from White's attacks. White beats Black by fixing him with pins, arm locks and strangles (see later). Black must disentangle himself from these various kinds of 'fixings' if he is to win. There are two ways it is done—before and after the 'fixing' is completed.

The best time to break out of any grappling technique is before it is applied! Look at photograph sequence 39 as an example. Before the final pin is applied Black maintains the momentum and rolls White off.

However, if the pin is applied, Black must have some plan to break out. White will, of course, be trying to hug his left chest as tightly as possible to Black's right chest. Therefore, Black has got to open up that space (see attacking and throwing spaces, page 12). By bouncing his hips and shoulders, and by rocking sideways, he will make some gaps between the two bodies, into which he can thrust or drive his hands and eventually his arms (see photographs 8(a)—(c)).

8 **A break-out**
(a) Black is attacking from the side. White bounces Black (using feet and hands).

(b) As he makes space between the bodies, White drives his left arm into the gap ...

(c) by pulling the right shoulder back and twisting, but still driving with the left arm. White can turn onto his front and so escape.

Once the arms are in, Black can turn his whole body into the space created and break out. It is not easy and it takes lots of energy, but with determination it is certainly possible.

Finally, instead of having Black starting on his elbows and knees, let the whole manoeuvre be done from a throwing situation. Black moves forwards or backwards and White attacks with taiotoshi or ouchi; Black steps out, sits and rolls over. White pursues, turns him over and then they can see who pins who!

Important Generalities

It is extremely important that novices are not allowed to think of throwing and grappling as if they are isolated in two kinds of boxes. The principles are the same for both and the two types of skills should be taught in the same way and learned at the same time.

The following is a simple example concerned with break-outs from pins. Earlier, I said the best way to get out of a pin was not to get into it; i.e. to anticipate it, to feel what is coming and not be there when it arrives! It is the same with throwing attacks. The black belt tries to anticipate a throwing attack; he feels the movement pattern that is being gradually built and then, just at the moment the opponent launches the throw, the target is not there. It is not easy, but with conscientious and sensitive training it can be done.

Let's return to attacking in throwing and grappling continuations. The novice's experience of learning how to throw and grapple at the same time could very easily be part of a black belt's tactical plan, too. A black belt could have the side pin (kuzureyokoshihogatame) as one of his contest winning skills. However, this black belt's throwing skills are not particularly good, so how does he get from a standing position into the horizontal one?

He pulls his opponent forwards, who moves very reluctantly (forwards). Our man quarter-turns and hooks his right leg in (but on the ground) so that he is very safe. The opponent, relieved, moves a step back. The attacker stabs his right leg forwards, without any more body turn, and only moves his left foot a little in order to get some kick/power into the action. Again, it is a very safe posture. The opponent stumbles and the attacker is on to him, pushing him over. The opponent tries to use the momentum generated to overturn and so end up on top in a winning position, but the attacker blocks the attempt, drives him onto his back and gets the winning pin.

When did the attack start? Too often, in too many text books, it is either actually said or strongly implied that the attack starts just before the completion. Of course that can happen—sometimes, but at black belt level it may well start several moves before the end, as in the above example (three pre-planned attacks before the terminal attack). That's why the novice needs to *start* his training in the same kind of conditions.

Back to the Contest

The two men are still trying to catch hold of each other's jacket. In the first few moments they are not very particular about where they hold—anywhere they can, anywhere the other man will let them. So, they grab and snatch, hands are knocked aside, bodies are twisted to take the jacket out of reach, and collars are jerked out of hands that do get a hold. It gets rough. Hands are being punched out: frustration is making the simple action a violent opening. Each man has a favourite grip, his strongest grip, the special grip that he must have to throw with. The other man knows it and so tries to keep away from that dangerous moment. He stalls, but in stalling he makes his own grip ineffective. Sooner or later one must risk the grip so that he can start his plan. As one holds, the other immediately hooks on. The tactics start.

WHAT DOES THE NOVICE NEED TO KNOW ABOUT GRIPS?

A lot! There are three basic wrestling styles that can be found in very slightly different forms throughout the world: (1) naked wrestling, in which the contestants have to hold the opponent's body as and where they can; (2) belt wrestling, in which the grip is restricted to holding just the belt (it can be specially designed); (3) jacket wrestling, in which the contestants can hold anywhere they wish in order to facilitate the skill. The range of skill offered by this last style, with an almost infinite choice of biomechanical holding positions, makes it easily the most sophisticated of the three types of wrestling.

The novice has to know that there are two general purposes of the hand grip:

1. The technical element: here the hands are 'hooks', attaching one body to another. The various forces generated by an attacker or a defender are transmitted to the opponent through the hand hold. They will also open and close the spaces between the bodies.

2. The tactical element: the hands are the forward radar station of the defending army. They feel when the opponent's muscle tensions are building up, revealing information about attacks and defences; they will assess the strong and weak points of the opponent's dispositions; the hands will break up attacks when they are made.

The starting, basic hold is where the left hand grips the opponent's right sleeve somewhere near the elbow, while the right hand holds the opponent's collar, somewhere near the base of the neck. The purpose is clear enough: the sleeve grip is to control the turning element in a throwing action. If the opponent wants to be twisted about his vertical axis, the right sleeve is pulled forwards and round so that the opponent will rotate. If the opponent needs to be rolled forwards (head over heels), the hand on the left collar is pulled down.

Any throw is a combination of these two hand grips. Some throws will need a dominant left hand (e.g. certain foot trips), others a dominant right hand (e.g. certain hip throws), while some will need equal emphasis (e.g. certain body throws). Sometimes the left hand will start the attack, sometimes the right will and sometimes their function will change about mid-attack. As competitive experience accumulates and attacks become more and more specialised, the grips will change to suit the favourite skill of the individual. He may hold both sleeves, or both collars, in the armpit, or the shoulder blade. Wherever the grip, the hands will be serving a special purpose: they will contribute a very subtle and important part of the attacking skill.

The novice should start with the standard hold, so that he gets an understanding of these functions: emphasis on the left hand, equal stress, emphasis on the right hand. Later on, of course, he can change to suit his own developing style. However, at whatever level of performance he is training, the competitor should know precisely what his hands are supposed to be doing and how he should be using them.

In this book it has been assumed that the two fighters have decided for the first couple of minutes or so to be cautious and only to try small score attacks. Two examples have been given, i.e. taiotoshi and ouchigake, but some more attacks are now needed. Remember, the requirements of small score attacks are:

1. They do not need full body weight commitment (see the section on ballistic movement in chapter 2).

2. The attacker must be very stable throughout the attack (of course, not *all* the time, just most of it!), i.e. he must have both feet on the ground at kake.

3. Only the minimum of body turn (by the attacker) is used (to help retain stability).

4. The spaces between the bodies are kept roughly constant (a slightly bent-arm distance).

5. Throwing power is kept sharp and is used only over short distances.

6. Attacking opportunities are when the opponent changes direction and thereby changes his line of concentration (a change of action must mean a change of thought).

7. Throwing and falling directions are the same (they differ if higher scores are needed; see chapter 2).

SOME MORE SMALL SCORE ATTACKS

Osotogari/gake

For the aficionado there are very significant differences between these two throws (gari/gake), but for the novice there is nothing to choose between them—they are the same.

White pivots on his right foot, briskly moves his left foot back somewhere near the opponent's left foot and then just as quickly the right foot/leg is hooked in behind the opponent's right leg (see photographs 9(a)—(d)). White pushes hard, with both hands, sideways. As, and if, Black

9(a)/10(a) The start of the attack.

9(b)/10(b) The opening attacking movement.

10(c) White's left leg moves forwards; his right leg hooks in behind Black's right leg ...

10(d) Black's right leg is 'pulled' forwards; Black falls ...

) White's left foot goes back; his
ht leg hooks in.

10(e) to his left side.

9(d) White's right leg 'pulls' Black's
right leg forwards, and Black falls.

stumbles, White 'runs' forwards,
maintaining the push sideways (to
Black's right).

The best attacking opportunity is
when Black is moving forwards or
to his left, so closing the space
between the bodies. If done when
Black is moving backwards or to his
right, the space is being opened
and it makes contact with the
hooking right foot very difficult.

Kouchigari/gake

White's left foot moves sideways
(to the left). He hooks his right foot
in low behind the opponent's right
leg, trying hard to split the legs
apart (see photographs 10(a)—
(e)).

The best opportunity again is when
Black is coming forwards or moving
to his right, for much the same
reason as above.

Note: When throws are similar, it is
a useful tactical practice to make
the opening attacking movements
the same so that the opponent
cannot guess which it is to be.

Kosotogari/gake

White steps sideways (to his right)
with his left foot (see photographs
11(a)—(e)). The right foot hooks in
behind Black's left heel, while both
hands push backwards and
sideways.

The opportunity presented is the
same as for the others.

Some comments A few so-called
traditionalists try to suggest that
there are some things called 'basic
techniques'. I do not know what the
phrase means and it always
confuses the novice. It seems that
these pseudo-traditionalists are
saying that there are certain
'techniques' which are common to,
or are a part of, all the other
techniques. That must be nonsense,
because how can a fast trip be a
part of a hip throw, or a leg throw

11 *Kosotegari/gake*

(a) The start is the same as in photographs 9(a) and 10(a), but now White's right foot moves slightly forwards, allowing the left foot to swing back.

be a part of a body throw? The only things that are common to all throwing—and, if it comes to that, grappling techniques as well—are arms and legs, but I do not think that is what they mean.

Of course there are no 'basic techniques', but there are plenty of 'basic principles'. Indeed, so far in this book 'basic principles' have played a major part in the discussions. It is essential to understand these so that when new attacks have to be 'invented' the competitor will have some idea of

(b) White's foot hooks behind Black's left leg.

(d) over his right foot.

(c) White's whole bodyweight push-drives Black sideways ...

(e) During the final stage White twists Black so that he lands on his back.

how to create the skill by using the various principles learned. This is why I have only very superficially outlined how to perform the low score attacks above. Once the novice has grasped the sequential aspects of each technique, i.e. where to put arms and legs and in roughly what order, he will need to apply thought and understand how, in fact, everything must be done at the same time.

For example, if a small score is made, the attacker may well decide spontaneously that he will attack immediately with some grappling technique. Which one will he use? How will he get down into a grappling position? Will he attack from the nearest or the furthest side? His answers will depend on the type of movement presented by the opponent (fast, slow, defensive, offensive), the spaces between the bodies (big or small), and the direction of movement (towards or away from the attacker). These are precisely the same factors that have to be considered when setting up a throwing attack. If the fighter has learned how to use these factors in an implementation of a principle, in one set of circumstances (e.g. throwing), it should be comparatively easy to transfer them to a different set of circumstances (e.g. grappling). It is this kind of spontaneous decision-making that makes judo exciting.

Conclusion

The contest has started; the fighters are finding their way. They have several sets of tactical plans, like cards, which they will use once they have decided how the opponent is going to play his hand.

They will have made several semi-committed attacks; some may have been for a small score (3 or 5) and others simply to test responses. None of the attacks will have been haphazard or lacking in thought and purpose (and therefore are not skill-less). On the results of these probing attacks each man will begin to decide how he is going to proceed to the middle phase of the match.

An Appendage

Here are some suggestions for organising an elementary class in judo.

1. The lessons do need to be planned. General or specific objectives should be decided and shown to the class. These objectives will be time-scaled, e.g. over 3 weeks, 2 months or one year.

2. The following patterns are based on the supposition that the class is to last an hour. If it is any longer it is difficult to maintain interest, to keep up a respectable learning rate, and to avoid exhaustion.

3. The general standard of physical competency must be known; is the group comprised mainly of young or old people, men or women, leisure-only orientated members or those wanting top competitive skills?

The standard can be established through a questionnaire when a new member joins the group, or through personal interview with the coach in charge, or through a combination of both.

Men and women can be dealt with in the same group, but it does create unique difficulties. Women usually do not have the same attitudes to wrestling as men; their movement patterns and motivations can differ considerably. The lesson plan will need to have a lot of flexibility to absorb these wide variations.

4. Much the same scale of attitudes will need to be worked out if there is a wide age range within the group. The older men (say, over 30) will require different considerations than the younger ones, depending upon their physical history (e.g. have they done much or very little sport before the judo class?). Class rhythms will have to vary to cater for all members. Generally speaking, the greater the variation in the group activity, the more interesting it is.

5. If children (e.g. before

puberty) are being included, their style of activity also needs special consideration. The range of intensity and activity should be wide (more so than for the adults), with lots of cross-body movements (e.g. reaching across the body centre line). There should be very little power/strength work and competition should be kept well within certain limited constraints. Children are not small adults: they require their own special considerations to satisfy their own special needs.

6. By and large, competition is used too often and too early in judo training (indeed, it is almost abused). It is accepted that the so-called 'grading system' (the awarding of coloured belts) is a perennial excuse for having it on the programme (more's the pity!) but, nevertheless, it should be kept to the minimum. Few novices enjoy or appreciate competition; it can be extremely violent and can—and does—switch many off from further attendance at the group. It also gets in the way of learning and improving. The pain and discomfort take an individual's mind off what he should be doing (improving his skills) and put it clearly on survival.

7. Judo does not have a good record of maintaining adult interest. The greater bulk of national associations' membership is children. There are, of course, many reasons for this, but certainly a major factor is lack of consideration for the individual. Each person must know that his requirements are appreciated and are being catered for, and that the lessons are prepared for *his*, not just anyone's, needs. Members must be made to feel they are a contributory part of the group. The relationships within the group and between the group and the coach (and other officials) are of vital importance. They will depend on things like understanding, tolerance, obligation, consideration and a developed, cultured atmosphere within the club or organisation.

Children have a great affinity with wrestling and, unless prevented by the system in which they find themselves, they enjoy it. The intimate body contact, particularly skin contact, is a very sensuous, pleasurable and necessary part of their physical education. The complex but simple movement patterns can generate both physical and mental maturity, and the group interactions can have many social benefits (e.g. by developing a sense of moral responsibility). However, these many advantages should not be exploited or misused by the adults, particularly by coaches and parents.

Allow the children to have their 'play' with judo, to learn in their own way, and to make up their own minds about staying with the sport (do not impose some adults' demands upon them, like winning contests!) Let them build their own relationships with judo and, who knows, they may stay with it when they have to move up into the senior group!

TWO BRIEF LESSON OUTLINES

Lesson 1: Patterns and Techniques

(a) *Warm up*. This should last about 5 minutes. It should include some flexibility exercises, i.e. those that extend the joint range. (N.B. Such exercises should *not* include 'beating into' the extreme of the joint range, since that is very dangerous.)

Other exercises should include quick changes of direction, wide ranges of body shape and changes of body orientation (e.g. cartwheels, tumbling and other similar gymnastic movements). There should be small physical 'tests' so they have to think about what they are doing, e.g. hop 3 times on the left leg, 5 times on the right leg. In short, the warm up should contain the same elements as the training session.

Long warm-up sessions should not be used as an excuse for not doing skill training.

Personal physical idiosyncrasies can be registered and precautions taken to ensure they are used to the best of the individual's advantage.

(b) *10 minutes' movement training* (similar to randori, but no throwing).

The class is encouraged to develop its own movement pattern (no attacks). There should be changes of direction (acute and oblique) and, if possible, changes of pace as the direction alters. The changes will be in certain recognisable parts within the overall pattern. They will be rehearsed so that consistency of pattern is achievable. In very early training days such patterns should be limited to 2 or 3 changes of direction only.

(c) *For 5 minutes.* The coach should suggest the type of throw that could be used at the changes. The description should be general, not specific.

(d) *For 5 minutes.* The group should try to work out, on its own, how these suggested attacks could be slotted into its own movement patterns.

(e) *For 15 minutes.* The coach should give specific instruction on how to improve the various attacks. He should move around the group, helping everyone individually.

(f) *For 10 minutes.* Limited free play (randori), restricted to the movement sets the group has created. The coach should be helping each pair as they are trying their attacks. Competition should not be mentioned!

(g) *For 10 minutes.* The coach shows how to convert all these attacks into newaza attacks, i.e. continuous movement from standing to ground.

(h) *For 5 minutes.* Free practice, but restricted to just those conversions learned. The coach will again be helping as members practise the various moves.

(i) *For 4 minutes.* Free practice (randori). Here the group can practise what they want. But, again, the coach should watch continuously and help individuals as they meet with difficulties.

(j) *For 3 minutes.* Warm down. Gentle exercises should be used to get the individuals into the showers without any great change of physical effort.

Some discussion on the evening's training may be held at the end. Did the group benefit from it? What have they learned? What was the time allocation like?

Lesson 2: Scores and Skills

(a) *Warm up.* Same as for Lesson 1.

(b) *For 10 minutes.* Practise the scores, i.e. how to land with regard to the score range 10, 7, 5, 3.

(c) *For 5 minutes.* Selection of throws for analysis, e.g. taiotoshi, sasaitsurikomiashi, tomoenage.

(d) *For 20 minutes.* The class can experiment with these throwing attacks so that they can differentiate/feel the difference between how they make each move. The thrower will feel the change in his body movement when making a 'three'-attack and a 'ten'-attack (how does the opponent minimise the score?). This will be a period of mutual help and co-operation.

(e) *For 5 minutes.* Practise the movements attempted in limited free play.

(f) *For 10 minutes.* The experiment can be repeated in newaza.

(g) *For 5 minutes.* The coach should discuss the various ramifications of such experiments.

(h) *For 4 minutes.* Free practice (randori). The group can do as it chooses.

(i) *Warm down.*

2 THE MIDDLE

As the battle moves into the middle phase, there is an imperceptible change of intent. The overture has finished and now the main movement of the symphony has started. The fighters are just syncretising their computerised information. They may well have watched each other before the contest began to discover if their opponent is left- or right-handed, how he stands up and sits down, how he walks (on his heels or toes), whether he turns naturally to the left or right, whether he takes long or short steps, and whether his movements are smooth or jerky.

Now they can also add the information they have uncovered in the opening phase. Are his responses fast or slow; does he move defensively or offensively? Are his attacks made from the 'inside' or from the 'outside'? (i.e. do the attacks come through the space between the arms (of the opponent) or do they come from the spaces outside the (opponent's) arms?) How does he handle space? Does the other man move around with patterns of movement that open and close all the spaces, so giving plenty of chances to attack with a range of actions, or does he try to hold the space as constant as he can, so that he has maximum control over all evolving situations?

For the spectator the interest will depend upon how the fighters 'play their cards'. If both are 'space utilisers' there will be plenty of excitement. Each one will be moving fast and slow, trying to manipulate the spaces for his own benefit, which means lots of action.

If they oppose each other, i.e. one competitor tries to exploit the spaces while the other tries to maintain a constant relationship, it can still be exciting because it is fascinating to see who can impose his personality on the other through physical skills. The one who succeeds wins.

If both are trying to maintain a constant relationship, the match will be extremely boring. It means that neither man knows enough about the skills, so he is too afraid to attempt to manipulate the conditions of the match for his own ends.

Having now synthesised all this information, plans are made. Which spaces will be used for attack and which for defence? What throw has he got for that particular space relationship? Which attack will be used for the centre of the contest area; which for the edge? Will he use single attacks or combined attacks? If combined, which are first; which are last? How will he prefer to counter—early or late? He will need to answer and correlate these questions and many more in a couple of seconds.

As the intent changes, so does the movement syncopation; the beat changes as each man momentarily dominates. Suddenly, they seem to move sideways in unison; one moves as if to attack, the other immediately responds by moving slightly backwards. The first man, feeling the spaces open, makes a full, committed attack; the second man now closes the space very fast and begins a counter-attack just as the other man's attack has begun. The first man instantly reverses his movement and in the process launches a different type of attack on the opponent's forward movement. The latter responds by violently throwing himself sideways out of the line of attack, which not only blocks the throw but screws the opponent round off his feet so that he falls over, landing on his hands and knees. The other man jumps down onto his shoulders, trying to find an arm lock, whereupon the opponent stands up with him still clinging onto his shoulders. The referee quickly steps forwards and stops the action to prevent either competitor injuring himself.

All that will take a couple of seconds or so. What can the novice learn from this fast interaction of skills?

MOVEMENT TRAINING

So that a point can be made, let us say there is a simple formula: skill = technique + movement (around the mat). By and large, when judo was being taught in the past this factor of movement was never considered. Whether it was forgotten or (more likely in my opinion) it was not understood, is not known, but what is evident is that only technique was ever taught. It was assumed the novice would discover and learn the movement by himself, once he had learned the technique. This is doubtful, of course, because the movement factor is the more difficult of the two. To add to the complexity, it is the movement which will largely dictate the type of attack used; if the novice does not understand that, skill improvement will take a long time. It is possible to make technique dictate a movement pattern (that is what usually happens at the present, anyway), but it takes a long time and does not produce the best results. (Look at the contemporary champions' range of skills.) So, why not teach movement first? A good question! Let's try it!

However, some general principles must be recognised first.

1. Attacking opportunities will only emerge from the ever-changing relationship between the two competitors. If they try to maintain the same relationship and keep the spaces between them constant in training, nothing will happen. Skill will not develop or improve; no one will throw the other and in many ways that will please the novice (he will not have to suffer the pain or the indignity of falling down). Yet in the long run, if skill does not grow, it may well discourage him from staying in the club.

Novices must move around as freely as apprehension and fear will allow. They should change the distance between the shoulders, between the chests, and between the hips and the feet as much as possible. They must feel the rhythm of free fluid movement.

2. They should not jerk into stiff defensive positions. When one novice twitches in an effort to make a throw, the other will tend to 'bury' his feet in the mat and stiffen his whole body against the shock to come. That must be shown to be a mistake. When an attack is made, the other novice should try to move around and avoid the movement. To 'jerk-stop' is to lose!

If an attack is blocked by such an action, it is the kind of response a skilful attacker wants, for now he can control his opponent's movement. By 'freeze-framing' the defence, all variables are eliminated, so making the job of throwing easier.

By learning to move around an attack, not only does it mean there is a wider range of variables (thus making the throw harder to complete) but it becomes the basis for a good countering skill later on.

3. *Movement between attacks is more important than the attack itself.* One often hears 'Old John has a terrible technique, but he always wins!' It is said in a tone of great mystery and incomprehension. It is, in fact, only to be expected, since the individual

12 A general starting position from behind the opponent
The legs do not squeeze but provide a firm grip, so allowing White's hands to do whatever technique is needed.

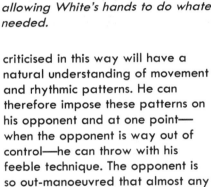

13 Wakigatame
(a) Black attacks with a top-pin. White begins to move under the right arm.

criticised in this way will have a natural understanding of movement and rhythmic patterns. He can therefore impose these patterns on his opponent and at one point—when the opponent is way out of control—he can throw with his feeble technique. The opponent is so out-manoeuvred that almost any throwing action would take him over and down.

4. The same idea, of course, applies in grappling. Try to maintain continuous body and weight relationships and not only will skill remain minimal but all will become extremely tedious. Ground work can be very exciting if approached through the idea of constant change in body relationships (I have often heard it called 'physical chess').

STRANGLES AND ARM LOCKS

The first thing to notice about these techniques is that they can only score 10 (ippon). They either work or they don't: there are no 3's, 5's or 7's! Many fighters do not like this aspect of these techniques, preferring pins where it is possible to score all four numbers, whereas others, of course, do prefer the all-or-nothing approach.

There are two kinds of strangles: one from the front, one from the back. There are also two kinds of arm locks; both are supposed to be applied to the elbow joint: when the arm is straight and when it is bent (in the latter case, due to the human anatomy the elbow cannot be isolated from the shoulder joint, so when the elbow is locked, so is the shoulder).

In strangles, pressure is applied to the neck, usually by a scissor action of the arms (see later). Either the windpipe is squeezed (a painful business) or the carotid artery at the side of the neck is squeezed (not so painful, but much more dangerous). Too much of this done too often can do damage to the brain (just like knockouts in boxing). It is a factor that should be particularly remembered in training. Participants should not be allowed to strangle each other into unconsciousness. Similarly, if locks are jerked on, permanent damage can be done to the elbow joint, and so that sort of application in training should be banned. On all occasions training partners should be given the greatest consideration.

(b) As he 'dives' out from under, White picks up Black's right arm ...

(c) and snaps on another type of straight arm lock.

General Principles

To make the application of locks and strangles effective, the opponent's body must be held under control. Without that it is fairly easy to break away from such attacks.

To retain control the legs must, somehow, be wrapped around the opponent and then fixed together in such a way that they cannot be forced apart. Look at photograph 12, but remember the rule (Article 28b xiii): 'To apply leg scissors (dojime) to the opponent's trunk, neck or head' (is not allowed), i.e. you can cross the legs, but you cannot squeeze with them.

Should the legs be wrapped around before or after the technique is applied? It will usually depend upon the particular skills of the individual. If his skill is general and he has no particular preference for locks, strangles or pins, he will generally lock his legs on first. This allows him to go for anything the situation draws out of the opponent. If he is a specialist, preferring locks or strangles above the other two, he may well get the hands in position first, and then hook the legs in afterwards.

Choice of technique will also depend upon the individual's style of movement. If it is fast, with flair, he will choose locks; if it is tenacious, with power, he will opt for strangles; and if it is powerful, but cautious, he will probably go for pins.

The Skills of Strangles and Locks

The easiest, and the best, time for using lock and strangle skills is when one fighter for some reason stumbles and falls down, probably landing on a knee. The other man leaps forwards, seizes a momentary set of circumstances and slams on an arm lock. (Novices can try to invent similar attacks of their own.)

The same kind of idea applies when both are wrestling on the ground. An attack always creates a weak point in the attacker's defence. At the very instant the attack is made, the opponent attacks and scores (is it a counter?). Look at photographs 13(a)—(c).

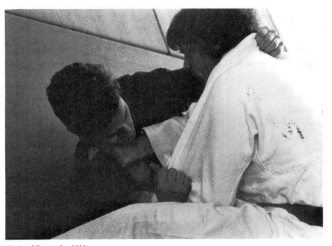

14 *Katajujijime*

(a) White moves in. Black reacts: he reaches up with his left hand and grabs White's back collar.

(b) White slides his right hand into Black's right collar ...

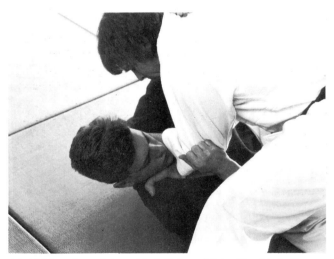

(c) White then drives his left hand into Black's left collar (now his arms are crossed). By pulling Black's head up, he applies the strangle.

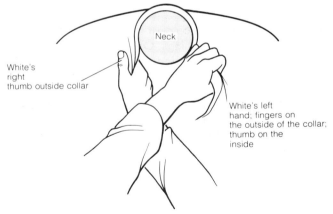

White's right thumb outside collar

Neck

White's left hand; fingers on the outside of the collar; thumb on the inside

(d) Katajujijime. To apply a strangle, drive both elbows downwards.

Black attacks with a pin; as he does so White comes out from under the arm and scores with an arm lock.

Again, look at photographs 14(a)—(c). The man on the ground, Black, reaches up to pull White's head down (so that he can roll him over). White holds Black's right collar with his right hand and then thrusts his left hand into Black's left collar. Both elbows are pushed down.

The coach can teach as many techniques of locking and strangling as he wishes, but it is the learner who has to convert them into a skill. So, in the learning situation the novice must be presented with as many different sets of circumstances as possible. With promptings and suggestions from the coach, the novice must find his own ways of doing things. Only by this means can he develop personal skills.

Back to the Contest

The middle phase of the match is where the big scores are usually made. All the information that can be known has been gathered together. Energy and power are at their peak, although after a few more minutes they will begin to wane, as concentration and tension sap the vital sources. Each man is completely keyed up to attack on the instant the right set of circumstances appears. He is willing this to happen and is manoeuvring as cunningly as possible to make sure it does.

There are pulls and pushes; some are very powerful, some are violent and others are so subtle and gentle that the opponent hardly registers them (but he will still, nevertheless, respond to them). Both hands work together, or each hand works separately, to elicit some reaction from the other man. Threatening moves will be made for big throws and distractions (hand holds changed, or arms moved from above the opponent's arms to below them) will be tried for the small throws. 'Psychological warfare' will also be attempted (false injury suffered, shouts and frightening noises made). Any combination of all these 'tricks' will be used to try to shatter—just for a moment—the concentration of the opposition. In that instant a major attack, with full body weight commitment, can be launched. Let's have a look at a few of these possible attacks, starting with the techniques.

Point 1 to remember: There are two basic ingredients in any throwing action: speed and power; the proportion of each will depend upon the ratio of speed and power in the general movement pattern before the attack is made. For example, if both fighters are moving slowly, cautiously but defensively, with lots of power to stop anything happening, any attack used to overcome such a situation will need far more power than speed. If both are moving easily, trying to exploit fast-evolving situations, the attack will require more speed than power. The more power needed, the closer the two bodies will have to be locked together (to ensure maximum transfer of that power); the more speed needed, the less contact there has to be between the bodies.

15 A beginner's ipponseoinage
(a) White prepares to attack.

(b) White's right foot moves forwards, his left foot swings ...

(c) back between Black's feet as White drops onto his right knee.

(d) If White only partly turns, he throws Black to his (White's) right.

(e) If a half turn is made, then Black goes forwards.

(f) If more than a half turn is used, Black falls to his (White's) left side.

Note: the advantages of each will depend upon a particular competitive situation, and therefore each will generate different ground work (newaza) tactics.

IPPONSEOINAGE

This is a throw for a slow, near static situation, where both men are moving very cautiously and defensively. If success is to be achieved, every move has to be executed with the utmost precision and with the maximum body contact to ensure the greatest amount of power transference possible. The attacker's inside arm (the right arm) is got rid of, so allowing the fullest contact. With most other orthodox throws, the inside hand retains the grip on the collar throughout the whole throwing action. That's fine, if a lot of body control is needed, but it can interfere with body contact if more power is required. Therefore, with ipponseoi the inside arm is thrown underneath the right arm of the opposition, so the bodies can be locked tightly together.

The whole of the attacker's body weight is driven into the direction of the throw by the left leg; it is this leg that generates the power. The body is kept straight with a twist coming up from the floor through the hips. (In the 'good old days' a judo fighter was taught to throw the opponent straight forwards, by turning his own body round through 180 degrees, bending straight forwards and pulling the man right over his head or back. This is a very dangerous way of throwing, for it can exert great strain on the thrower's back. Many of the past judo generations had to give up the sport and/or suffer much in middle age because of this bad biomechanical performance advocated by ill-trained coaches. Sad to say, it can still happen.)

There is a wide range of throwing direction for this throw. Orthodoxy suggests that the opponent can be thrown only to his front (forwards). The imaginative performer (the champion) throws anywhere, from forwards to backwards! The actual direction will depend upon the stance and foot position of the opponent.

A rough guide would be that if the opponent's right foot is *back*, he would be thrown sideways (to his right); if the foot is *forward* he is thrown backwards; if the feet are *square* he is thrown forwards.

The way the opponent moves will usually decide where the feet are when the attack is made. Moving sideways or in a circular manner usually means the feet are square; when forwards the right foot is usually forward and when moving backwards the foot is back. There is plenty of scope for the way this throw can be used in spite of the very limiting circumstances in which it is done. It is a throw that needs a great deal of courage, as stops and counters are comparatively easy for the opponent to make. Therefore, it also requires discipline and lots of control and patience.

How does the novice learn it? Look at photographs 15(a)—(f). See how White turns, drops onto his right knee and feels/rolls his partner across his back. During the early stages of learning Black can simply roll over the proffered back and onto the mat. White can then sort out the different throwing directions. In photographs 15(d), (e) and (f) the kneeling action is the same. The difference is the amount of turn made by the attacker. The general point he has to appreciate is that good class fighters do not like to turn round very far, since it provides too good a countering opportunity. This is why experienced performers tend to throw sideways or backwards, where the need to turn is not so great.

The style and the extent of turning should then be integrated with the movement patterns. White moves forwards, steps across his body with his right foot, pivots, turns and pulls himself hard into his partner, dropping onto his right knee as he

16 Avoidance

(a) White attacks with ipponseoi. Black moves round the front, avoiding the drive.

(b) Black moves away smoothly to continue the action.

(c) As White makes almost the same attack, Black now moves behind White ...

(d) and again smoothly continues the action.

does so. He then tries it as he moves backwards, in circles and in any other way he can think of—the more the better!

AVOIDING AND COUNTERING

Because ipponseoinage is such a 'slow' throw, avoiding actions and countering attacks are fairly easy for the opponent to organise. Black can usually step over or move round the attack, to the front or behind. See photographs 16(a)—(d). It is for this reason that White has to drive his right shoulder hard into Black's shoulder (see photographs 17(b) and 18). It helps to stop this kind of avoidance. Black's right arm must not be allowed to get on top of White's right shoulder. If so, it will facilitate counters considerably.

17 *Ipponseoinage*
(a) At the start all four hands are defending and attacking at the same time. To get full body contact in such a situation is very difficult. To free one side White frees his right hand and leaps into this tight position, swinging his hips right through

so that ...
(b) Black is thrown across his back. Note White's driving left leg.

18 It is very important to note how these two shoulders are locked together. Study carefully and copy carefully.

General comments When the matter of chest contact , i.e. the need to transfer power and how it is to be done, is understood by the novice he will be able to utilise that information in some other throws. For example, if taiotoshi is to be used in the same set of circumstances, i.e. slow and powerful, it, too, must contain these same elements. The right elbow is thrust under the opponent's left arm, the hips are swung through (as for ipponseoi) and the range of throwing directions is almost as wide as ipponseoi.

UCHIMATA AND HARAIGOSHI

This type of throw, where the attacker balances on one leg while he throws, is obviously for the middle range of speed and power. Both men are moving around, somewhat faster than for ipponseoi; both are changing shape and the spaces between the bodies are changing continuously. Body weights will be moving around the 'feet base', changing from heels to toes and to edges of the feet, and back again. It is during these various changes that an opportunity will be created for one man to try his luck. He will need to move fast, because he has to 'catch' one of the changes as the opponent stands up straight, leans forwards, moves a shoulder forwards or backwards, or as he

changes pace—for that is the weakest moment, however small the change is.

Haraigoshi, see photographs 19(a)—(c), is a throw that tries to take advantage of the opponent leaning forwards as he changes direction of movement (particularly from forwards to backwards). The right foot steps forwards, the left foot swings back and the right leg sweeps back and up, knocking the opponent's leg out from under him. The attack demands confidence and very accurate timing. If the latter is wrong, even by a split second, a counter is bound to result because the attacker, standing on one leg, is unstable.

However, some precautions can be taken to avoid such an occurrence.

In photograph 19(b) note how the left foot is kept outside Black's base (foot area). This ensures White's weight is driving into the

19 *Haraigoshi*
(a) (top) White and Black move cautiously sideways towards the camera.
(b) (middle) Black changes direction, half turns and moves away from the camera. White cross-steps, gets his left leg well back near Black's left foot, and swings the right leg ...
(c) (bottom) out, back and up into the top of Black's thigh, lifting Black's legs out from under him.

direction of the throw. Notice how White's right hand is pushing Black's head out and down, and how he is keeping the right elbow up to facilitate the push. See how White's left hand is pulling in close to the body, causing Black's right shoulder to move forwards. This hand action should start as the left foot swings back to drive, but remember that much has gone on before the attacking movement was started. White will need to manoeuvre Black into the leaning forward position—Black will not stand still for White's benefit. White will have to move Black around quite a lot if he is going to get a chance to attack.

Uchimata has much the same action as haraigoshi. It is a middle speed range throw and therefore does not need much body contact, but the attacker's right hip must be in close contact with the opponent's left hip and his left foot must be on the outside of and close to the opponent's left foot. The sweeping leg of haraigoshi (hence the name) is used to knock the opponent's legs and hips out from underneath him. It looks simple enough, but it is extremely difficult. The main problem is that the sweep 'breaks' the hip/leg line and thereby can stop the throw happening. For success the point of contact of the swinging right leg must be very accurate, about 6" below the 'skin line', i.e. 6" below the point at

(a)

(c)

(b)

(d)

which the leg joins the hip. Uchimata avoids this problem by the swinging leg going up between the opponent's legs, making sure there is complete contact with the opponent's hips. The swing, however, is sideways and takes the opponent's left leg sideways which, in turn, will pull the right leg along

20 Uchimata
(a) The attacking position. Note that Black's right foot is well back.
(b) White moves in with only a quarter turn; he pulls hard down and in with his left hand.
(c) Black is thrown sideways over the edge of his right foot.
(d) White falls over Black because of full weight commitment.

21 Uranage
(a) White gets ready to attack.

(b) White thrusts the whole of the right side of his body forwards, getting his right foot past Black's left foot.

(c) White moves his left foot well forwards, allowing great body twist. There is **no** lift, only twist.

with it, thereby taking both legs out from under him (see photographs 20(a)—(d)).

Notice a couple of points which are similar to haraigoshi: the left foot is outside Black's foot base, and the hand action is much the same. Different points are: White's body does not have to turn so much (this facilitates the *sideways* sweep of the right leg) and the direction of throw is not the same (haraigoshi

throws are made very much forwards, whereas uchimata throws are to the side).

Movement opportunities are similar in both throwing attacks.

Remember that none of these points are sacrosanct: they will be changed to suit the size and the personality of the thrower and the set of circumstances selected in which to make the attack.

SUTEMIWAZA/BODY THROWS

Traditionally sutemiwaza is translated as 'sacrifice throws'. Not only is this a travesty of the meaning of the word 'sutemi', but, worse still, it conjures up a totally wrong image of what the throw should be like. Sacrifice has all kinds of negative connotations, whereas the throw demands very positive action throughout.

(d) Black is dropped behind White.

(e) Note the position of White's left hand. It is clamping the two bodies very tightly together — just like ippon seoi.

This type or group of throws utilises or exploits the force developed by making the (attacker's) body drop down in a very purposeful way. It is that force which is used to throw the opponent. There are two main sub-divisions in this group; one is used in the same general conditions as ipponseoi, e.g. slow movement, strong action, while the other type is used in conditions preferred by haraigoshi and uchimata, i.e. the middle range of speed and strength. The first sub-group of sutemiwaza has a twisting body action to develop the necessary power, whereas in the second the opponent's head and shoulders are pulled down and then he is rolled forwards over his feet. Let's look at a typical throw from each set (there is insufficient space to deal with the many variations in these groups).

The Twister Type

White slides his right hand round Black's waist and grabs a fistful of belt (somewhere near Black's right hip); the right foot steps forwards and wide. See photographs 21(a) —(e). White then moves his left foot as far forwards as he can, ensuring there is a tight fit between the two bodies, from hip to armpit.

It is the same kind of contact as in ipponseoi. White's left hand then pushes into Black's belt, in front of his stomach. With a massive drive off the left foot, White's body twists hard and fast to his right.

Because of the close contact of the bodies—maintained by White's gripping right hand—the whole twist is transmitted to Black, who is flung behind White's feet. It is a fast, powerful and frequently painful throw, but it is very effective.

This type of throw can be used offensively or defensively; it is often used as a counter-throw. Like ipponseoi it requires courage and much discipline of movement. The attacking opportunity is, of course, at the moment of change, particularly in direction but also in postural shape (hence its popularity as a counter).

Points to observe Notice how far White's left foot moves forwards (to provide the power base) and that White does *not* land on his back, but on his *front*. There is very little, if any, lifting action in this throw; it is all twist, thus avoiding back strain and injury.

The Roller Type
Look at photographs 22(a)—(d). The left arm pulls the head and shoulders down. The right hand, pushing up into the opponent's stomach, helps to rotate the

22(a)

(b)

(c)

(d)

opponent, while the turning and falling body weight provides the power to complete the rotation.

Try the action: White reaches down Black's back and grabs a fistful of jacket; White's left foot steps wide and the right hand thrusts hard into Black's stomach as the right foot goes between Black's legs. That foot generates the power to complete the rotation. Again, White must *not* land on his back but on his *front*. See photograph 22(d). (Here tradition tells the attacker to land on his back. This not only reduces power to zero, but allows the opponent to do unpleasant things to him, e.g. to fall on top of the thrower in the most painful of ways!)

There are many versions of this throw. The most famous is

22 *Ukiwaza*

(a) The starting position. Notice the position of White's left hand: it is to control and pull down Black's head.

(b) White's left foot steps forwards very deeply, allowing the necessary body control.

(c) White's right foot moves very far forwards, generating the dynamic power for the right hand to rotate Black.

(d) The power generated by White is sufficient to rotate both bodies, which means that White ends up on top of Black.

45

23 Tomoenage
(a) Start of the attack.

(b) White jumps forwards, driving his right foot into Black's left groin. White's left foot moves wide, making White fall to his right.

(c) White is now across Black's feet.

(d) White spins Black over sideways with a pull on Black's right sleeve.

(e) White use the momentum to turn himself over so that he lands on top of Black, as in (f).

(f) White should now be in control.

tomoe-nage (stomach throw). Here the thrusting right hand, as described above, is replaced by one or two feet. As usual, once the general notion is understood, i.e. head down, legs up, the budding champion can make up his own model (see photographs 23(a)—(f)).

The movement opportunity for this roller type of sutemiwaza is much like that for haraigoshi and uchimata when there is a fast change of direction or body shape. The skilful competitor mixes the openings (to attack) in such a way that the opponent does not know if he is about to use a fast 'one-legged throw' or a quick 'body throw'. Remember, an uchimata uses less body turn than haraigoshi but more than a roller sutemi, so the opponent could easily be confused as to which is which.

24 Sasaitsurikomiashi
(a) Starting the attack.

(b) White steps well forwards with his left foot, thereby getting the two bodies close together.

(c) White twists strongly to his right, pulling his right hand down, forwards and round. White's blocking right foot prevents Black from stepping forwards with his left foot.

(d) The momentum swirls White round so that he finishes over Black.

ASHIWAZA/FOOT TRIPS

The Japanese language does not differentiate between foot and leg (the 'leg/ashi' extends from the tip of the toes to the hip joint). When discussing judo technique this can be confusing sometimes.

Restricting the meaning of ashiwaza to foot trips, there can be said to be two types, each dealing with a different mix of speed and power. The first sub-group is mostly concerned with power, but with some speed, which overlaps the fast range of the haraigoshi type of attack. Here the opponent's feet are trapped (not allowed to move) and he is pulled or pushed over the fixed feet. The second sub-group involves speed and virtually no power at all. Here the opponent's feet are simply and quickly kicked out from under him.

Sub-group 1

Look at photographs 24(a)—(d). White steps well forwards with his left foot. This allows him to get his hips close to Black's, but without the force of actual contact. The right foot is put across Black's left foot (preventing him from moving it) with a body twist, which is a very similar move to that in the first type of body throw (but without the following fall down). White throws Black to White's right side.

Points to look for When White is twisting to throw, he must be 'falling' to his right side, *not* his left (see photograph 24(c)). It is best if White's right hand is holding 'high', i.e. behind Black's neck, so that as the body twists the right hand can pull hard, down and round. This reinforces the twisting action of the body. White's left hand is pushing Black's right arm up and round, to back up the action of White's right hand.

Notice that there is a great similarity between this type of throw and the first of the body throws, although here the body does not fall to the ground. The difference is due to the degree of speed and power necessary in the two throwing circumstances. With body throws greater power is needed, and speed is much slower.

Sub-group 2

As the opponent moves fast and lightly the attacker takes one or both feet out from under him by sweeping his legs away (see photographs 25(a)—(d)).

It appears one of the easiest throws of the whole judo repertoire, but it is, in fact, one of the hardest. Because of this apparent simplicity, many years ago it was the first throw to be taught to beginners. The usual result was great frustration, great disappointment and great bruises on the shins!

Let's have a look at some of the difficulties.

As the opponent moves his right foot forwards, backwards or sideways (towards the left foot), the attacker steps sideways with his right foot, while the left sweeps the opponent's right foot towards his left. With no foot or leg to stand on, he falls down!

25 Okuriashiharai
(a) White drives Black back with a strong push on his left shoulder.

(b) Black responds by moving his left foot back, and allows his right to follow it.

(c) White steps well forwards with his right foot and sweeps both Black's feet with his left foot.

(d) Black drops straight down.

Points to look for White pulls or pushes Black's left arm in the direction that he intends to sweep the foot. White's body must be kept up straight throughout the attacking action. The two bodies do not have to get any closer than they were at the beginning of the attack.

Movement opportunities When an attack has been made, but it proved to be unsuccessful, the attacker tends to retreat very fast to get back to the safety of his own territory. It is an excellent time for a foot trip attack. Medium range speed attack also usually causes the opponent to move very quickly out of the 'line of fire' and this is another good opportunity for a foot trip attack.

HANDS-ONLY THROWS

This penultimate set calls for the most skill. Only the slightest body weight is used, and the only power really available is in the hands. General movement is in the middle to fast range. The attacker manoeuvres both bodies into a certain relationship; by a feint with his hands (to throw in one direction) he makes the opponent stiffen one side of his body against the 'attack' direction. Then, by exploiting that rigidity (as a kind of fixed point of reference), the attacker rotates the opponent the other way with the use of just his hands. This is the most exciting form of throwing there is: it requires no power, only complete harmony of one man's movement combined with another's. Sensitivity and awareness of the most subtle actions lead to this very special kind of throwing. When I was a young fighting man, my teacher made me practise these throws, and nothing else, for many months. Eventually I was able to throw 2nd and 3rd Dans with these techniques. I can still remember the almost sublime pleasure it gave me —not the beating of an opponent, but the sheer joy of being able to move into the skin of another man and make him do what I wanted him to do.

NO-HANDS THROWS

Lastly, there is the epitome of 'doing without doing'. ('Doing without doing' is a famous Zen maxim. Very briefly, it refers to that well-known performance of a champion: he can only perform his best skill when he is not trying to do it.) The opponent launches an uncontrolled force (it can be through anger, violence, ineptitude or ignorance). The 'defender', although he hardly justifies the name in such circumstances, simply gets out of the way of this crazy force. Since there is no resistance, the opponent falls over, thrown by his own momentum (see photographs 26(a)—(d)).

26 *Wakiotoshi*
(a) It must be imagined that Black is rushing at White, almost (but not quite) out of control.

(b) White grabs Black's head and belt and — stepping to the side — simply lies down in front of Black's movement.

(c) Black begins to roll over White's blocking body.

(d) Again, the generated momentum ensures that White can finish on top of Black.

51

Such occurrences are, of course, very rare, but they do happen. Jijoro Kano shows it quite clearly in his itsutsu-no-kata and it can be seen occasionally when one competitor pushes violently forwards and the other drops and spins round, making himself into a ball over which the other man falls. Such a 'throw' is often called ipponseoinage!

In figure 2 I have tried to show the paradox of how all these throws flow from one into another. By modifying the famous yin yang symbol, I want to indicate there is a continuum of speed to power, but the two elements do join up and the throws can slide round it, overlapping in many areas. There is a similarity here with the traditional interpretation of the 'black belt gyro system' in judo.

The absolute beginner wears a white belt. He moves round to the black belt segment and then on round to the absolute master's stage, which is also a white belt: it symbolises that the 'thoughtless' spontaneous skill of the master is next to the unknown, innocent spontaneity of the novice. Both men are 'doing without doing'.

There is no particular or single way of classifying any one throw. They can be, and are, modified greatly to suit different circumstances and personalities. Throws such as taiotoshi are like Spitfires in World War II: by changing their wing shapes, tail planes, engines, cockpits or undercarriages, they could be used for almost any job — as fighters, photo reconnaissance, tank busters, carrier aeroplanes and yet in essence they still remained Spitfires. A taiotoshi can be a hip throw, a hand throw, a leg throw or a body throw, but it still remains a taiotoshi. The conversions need imagination and a comprehensive knowledge of the trade of fighting

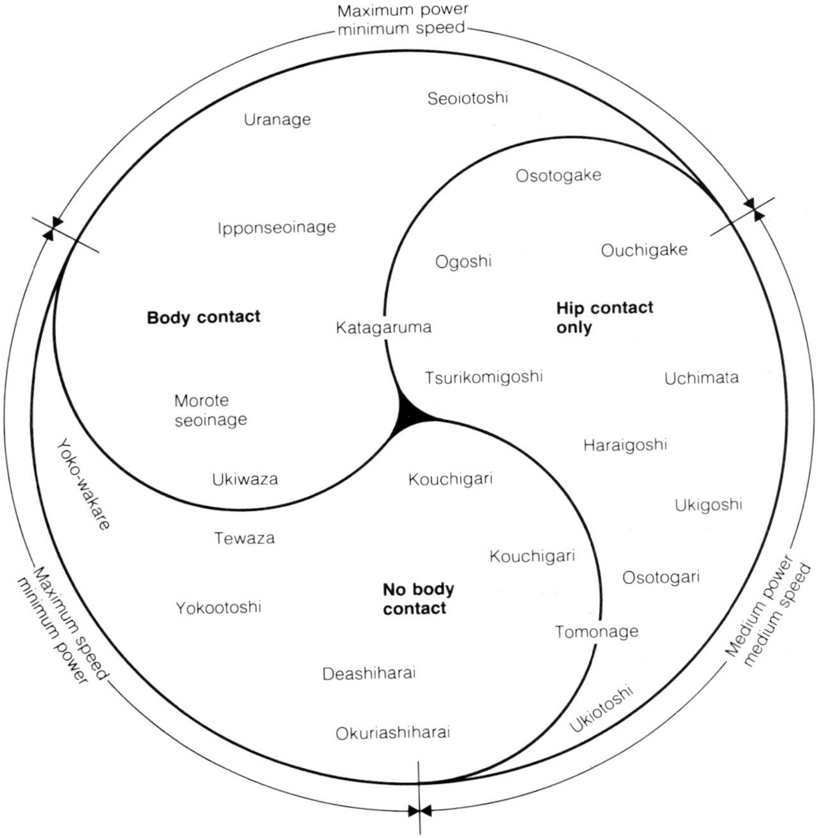

Maximum power
minimum speed

Seoiotoshi

Uranage

Osotogake

Ipponseoinage

Ogoshi

Ouchigake

Body contact

Hip contact only

Katagaruma

Tsurikomigoshi

Uchimata

Morote seoinage

Haraigoshi

Ukiwaza

Kouchigari

Ukigoshi

Tewaza

Kouchigari

No body contact

Osotogari

Yokootoshi

Tomonage

Yoko-wakare

Deashiharai

Ukiotoshi

Maximum speed minimum power

Okuriashiharai

Medium power medium speed

Fig. 2
Throws related to speed and power. The names are not in fixed positions. Many, but not all, could move around their general area; a few could move into different areas.

within the rules, which any good coach, to say nothing of a fighter, should have.

Back at the Contest

Each man is struggling to impose his tactical plan on the other. The conflict sways from side to side as first one man dominates and then the other. Favourite 'big guns' (throws) have been fired, but so far with little success.

To make the struggle more interesting and more personal, we should identify with one of the contestants, so that we can share his successes and failures. This is a stimulating ingredient when watching a match, although actual physical identification is not always easy in judo, as both men wear the same sort of white kit. All that distinguishes one from the other is a sash, either red or white. Since these are frequently covered by a loose jacket, it can still be confusing. However, we will back Red, since it's a good colour!

Red feels desperation beginning to overwhelm him. He tried taiotoshi in the corner, where he had hoped the restriction of the corner would make the attack effective, but the opponent had stopped it. Now, what to do? Quite obviously the opponent is not going to be fooled by simple tricks and so a complex tactical scheme will have to be implemented. Red Sash utilises the tactical knowledge he has acquired during training.

A word about judo kit Judo kit has remained exactly the same for the last hundred years. It is the product of a long-gone social milieu. The rules say (Article 3): The contestant shall wear judogi (judo costume) with the following conditions:

(a) It shall be strongly made in cotton or similar material, in good condition (without wear or tear).

(b) It shall be white or off-white, without excessive markings.

The various measurements, e.g. length of sleeve and trousers, are minutely defined. However, judo kit is now a complete anachronism and it is in desperate need of redesign and reappraisal. What is needed today is a coloured kit, one by which different groups of competitors can be identified (e.g. country, club or team). It should be designed to stay on the body of the athlete when 'the battle rages' and it should not produce the effects of being in a sauna when it comes to training and competing in the heat. After my advocating this for about 20 years, the European Judo Union is to experiment with the idea.

WHAT ARE TACTICS AND HOW CAN THEY BE CREATED?

Let us imagine that Red Sash is a 'throwing man'. He does not like grovelling on the mat in the dust, but wants to make his wins with big throws, which is the true spirit of judo. He, like some others, feels it is the only way to win and so neglects all the other ways of winning that can be found in the rule book. The audience, comprising mostly judo enthusiasts, recognises his spirit and so they all support Red Sash. Because of this bias in his skill development, Red Sash's tactical planning will have a heavy emphasis on throwing, although groundwork situations will have to be allowed for. Certainly, White Sash is very slow and keeps letting his right hand drop down, indicating he may well be a groundwork man (the dangling hand is ready to grab a leg and turn Red Sash over so that he falls to the ground). Red Sash thinks he ought to step the pace up and make White change directions frequently so that he can block White's attacks, but it will also make Red Sash's ouchi—his best throw—more effective. Red Sash will have to keep Article 17 well in mind, however, for he must make it work for him.

Article 17—Entry into ne-waza (groundwork) 'The contestants shall be able to change from standing position to ne-waza (groundwork) in the following cases, but should the employment of the technique not be continuous, the referee orders both contestants to resume the standing position:

(a) When a contestant, after obtaining some result by a throwing technique, changes without interruption into newaza (groundwork) and takes the offensive.

(b) When one of the contestants falls to the ground, following the unsuccessful application of a throwing technique, the other may follow him to the ground or when one of the contestants is unbalanced and is liable to fall to the ground after the unsuccessful application of a throwing technique, the other may take advantage of his opponent's unbalanced position to take him to the ground.

(c) When one contestant obtains some considerable effect by applying a shime-waza (strangle) or kansetsu-waza (a lock) in the standing position and then changes without interruption to newaza (groundwork).

(d) When one contestant takes his opponent down into newaza (groundwork) by the particularly skilful application of a movement which although resembling a throwing technique does not fully qualify as such.

(e) In any other case where one contestant may fall down or be about to fall down, not covered by the preceding sub-sections of this article, the other contestant may take advantage of his opponent's position to go into newaza (groundwork).

Red Sash must be particularly careful about sub-section (b). White Sash will no doubt be ready to use this, with the slightest provocation, and Red knows he would then be in trouble. With luck, however, the referee may be biased towards a real 'thrower'. Much of the assessment of a 'take down' will depend upon such a bias; a 'traditional' referee will often prefer the 'true judo man', i.e. the thrower, and will penalise the grappler, whatever he does. White sash knows that, too, so his 'take down' will be very subtle (and will fool no one except the referee). White jumps forwards, turns in the air, lands on both knees in front of Red Sash (the 'do without doing' throw, see page 52) and hopes that Red Sash will stumble over him. Being trained in the 'old school', Red Sash just stands there and does stumble over White's tucked-up body. He puts his right hand down for support and White grabs it, pulls it in tight and rolls Red Sash over onto the ground. The referee is uncertain; should he stop the contest? While he is thinking, White Sash is already burrowing in for a pin.

The referee decides to let it go... the fight goes on.

A Few Principles that Emerge from the Struggle

1. You can never afford to lose concentration during a contest. Train to expect anything and everything at any time. Train never to be still, irrespective of whether you are standing up or lying down.

2. If you allow the opposition to gain the initiative, at any time, it is very difficult to get it back. Therefore, always fight to control the *next stage*, not to stop at the *present one*.

3. Train never to let your back touch the ground *at any time*. The good ground grappler will make sure you stay there, once you let your back touch!

4. In groundwork it is essential to know what is going on *all around you*. Train to see/think about what is behind your back (see page 63). Learn to feel/think the opponent's arm coming from behind your neck. Know where the opponent's legs are, even though you cannot see them.

What can the novice learn from all this? Groundwork (newaza) attacks do not start from a static situation. In the past when, for example, a pin (osaekomi) was taught, one novice was told to lie on the ground, and another was shown how 'to hold him down'. He would have plenty of time to think about what he was doing and would end up in the right place, but with no dynamic strength at all. The partner would have time to generate a lot of power, more than enough to throw the pinner off with no trouble. Both would wonder how such a facile 'hold' could hold anybody. It is not surprising that groundwork skills were so badly executed in the past.

Life is not like that, of course. Everything is in a state of flux and short supply. Whatever is on offer will need to be used for all its worth. The earlier the novice understands that, the quicker he will learn and improve. He must learn in a dynamic situation so that he can discover how to use his momentum to generate the power for the pin.

What should the novice learn first —pins (osaekomi), arm locks (kansetsuwaza) or strangles (shimewaza)? It does not matter really, as long as they are learned as a part of a general movement pattern. Each has its advantages and disadvantages. Pins are 'steady' and are often a good gamble; if the opponent breaks out of the pin, the attacker does not necessarily lose the winning position. If, on the other hand, the opponent breaks away from locks or strangles, the superior position is usually lost with it and the attacker must start from scratch again to build another plan of attack. Finally, as has been said already, locks and strangles can only score 10 (ippon), while pins can score 3, 5, 7 or 10.

Some simple locking and strangling techniques A general outline of locks and strangles has already been described. Here are some standard techniques that can be learned quite quickly: see photographs 27(a)—(g).

What would you do in a situation like this?

(a)

(b)

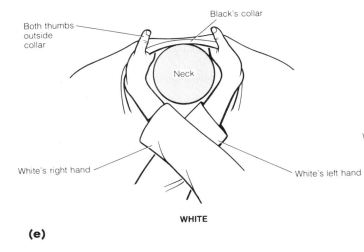

Both thumbs outside collar

Black's collar

White's right hand

White's left hand

Neck

WHITE

(e)

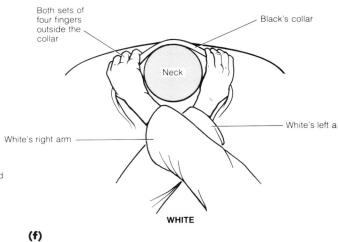

Both sets of four fingers outside the collar

Black's collar

White's right arm

White's left a

Neck

WHITE

(f)

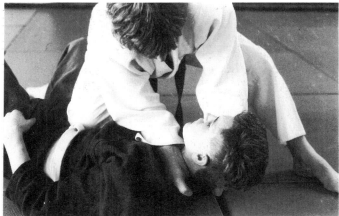

(d)

27 *Standard techniques*

(a) A 'down' udegarami, a bent-arm lock.

(b) An 'up' udegarami. **Note:** *White's body position should always control Black's general movements.*

(c) A standard straight arm-lock, udegatame.

(d) Katajujijime: a cross-arm strangle (see photograph sequence 14). **Note:** *White's controlling position.*

(e) A typical attacking position for gyakujujijme.

(f) A typical attacking position for namijujijme.

(g) White's right hand is deep in Black's left collar; his left hand is behind Black's head, forcing it forwards into the 'cutting' right wrist.

Remember, these skills can absorb a great deal of energy and power, and that is why they are usually used in the middle of the match. They are tough to apply in the last phase, because they are so exhausting.

Back to the Contest

Red Sash is now having to readjust his fighting plan. He got out of the groundwork exchange successfully, but only after a savage mauling. He does not want to repeat it, since he may not be so lucky next time. He now slows the pace down (by crouching low and holding his body weight slightly towards his heels), so that he has time to think. His 'big guns', the straight frontal attacks, are not having much success, because White Sash reacts too fast and stops most things before they are dangerous. Red Sash decides to give White Sash a taste of his own medicine. In the groundwork exchange, White Sash strung together a run of techniques ostensibly designed to tire, but more importantly to confuse Red Sash so that he could not 'see' when the final attack was launched. Red Sash quickly selects his tactical plan and immediately launches it: he pulls and pushes White Sash towards the edge of the fighting area. White responds instinctively by pushing back and moving towards the centre of the mat,

where he feels safe. Red Sash slams in with his ouchigake (both feet on the ground), which forces White Sash to move backwards towards the contest edge. However, sensing something amiss, White immediately changes direction to sideways. Red Sash is pleased; he allows a two-step time interval and then punches in a hard taiotoshi. White Sash, with a touch of desperation, quickly steps over the extended leg and moves away fast. Red Sash pursues him just as rapidly and attacks again with an ankle trip, okuriashiharai. White Sash feels it coming, stiffens slightly and tries to bury his feet into the ground. Red Sash, with only an imperceptible change of body movement, generates an ipponseoi against the fixed stance. White Sash finds himself going and is annoyed, because he knows that to stand still, to offer a fixed set of circumstances, is to invite a dangerous attack. He is 'flying', but the day is not lost—not by any means!

What can the novice learn? The novice will need to study the various throwing directions that each technique will dictate (probably with the aid of a good coach). He must learn that if he pushes harder with his left hand than his right, the opponent may well go in the way of the push. However, if he moves strongly to

his left, the opponent might move the opposite way. Such information is essential if he is to construct attacking sequences of his own.

The above linked attack is an example of the easiest kind. One man is doing all the attacks. In a highly skilled contest the opposition will be injecting his own throwing actions into the sequence, thereby providing counter moves. In such a match there can be a 'rally', as in tennis; there may be an attack, a counter, a counter-counter, a follow-up, another attack, and so on. It is a very exciting element within a judo contest.

Some concluding thoughts
Because of the anachronistic character of scoring in judo contests, there is little place for tactical development in the sport. This is a great pity and, without doubt, it is holding back the development of judo skills and hence the progression of the sport as a whole. The judo youth of today are expected to learn the same material that judo fighters of a hundred years ago had to learn. For those distant champions there may have been some relevancy in what they learned, but today this is no longer the case. It hampers and stultifies the skills that contemporary youth are trying to develop. Fortunately, however, there are a few inspired individuals

in every generation who break away from these ossified traditions and devise new skills and teaching methods to keep the sport moving. Without them we would have problems.

Judo competitors nurtured in a cobweb-strewn training programme have little idea of what to do once they are in an important contest, for they have been told nothing about skills or tactics, only about techniques. Therefore, they usually just stand there, making themselves as hard and rigid as they can, hoping the gods will smile on them and make the opponent attack first so they can counter. The gods smile on very few! This is why most judo matches are so dull, but sooner or later tactics will be taught properly and then judo matches will become as exciting as they possibly can be. It is true to say that if judo is presented properly, it is a very dramatic sport.

Tactics need studying. Hannibal was a great tactician and his battles can be studied with much benefit by the up-and-coming judo champion. Hannibal never fought where the enemy wanted to fight, only where *he* wished to fight. His victories at Lake Trasimene and Mons Calenus, although very different in tactical design, both used this principle in an ingenious way. However, Scipio, probably the only Roman who did beat Hannibal, would not take him on in battle until he had trained his army to beat Hannibal's tokuiwaza (favourite skill), the elephant. Japanese judo folk lore says that a fighter's favourite, and hence his strongest, attack is the weakest link in his defence. This seems to have been true for Hannibal. When the Romans countered the elephants, they ran amok among the ranks of the Carthaginians, causing great chaos and giving an easy opportunity for the Romans to win.

SOME TACTICAL BUILDING BRICKS

There are three main 'building bricks' about which a training judo man should know.

1. Direct Attacks

These are the various techniques (the straight throws and the ground-wrestling techniques) that are shown in most orthodox text books. The trouble is that they are always made to look so much easier than they really are; they are described very simply—put a foot here, a hand there and all is well—and so the layman imagines that is the only way they are done or, indeed, can be done. Unfortunately, this is not true. Any throw can be executed in many ways, and the feet and the hand positions can vary enormously. The direction of the throw can differ considerably, too, and alteration in body shape can change the pace at which it can be performed.

Indeed, the reason that any one throw becomes 'popular' (such as taiotoshi, uchimata, ippon-seoinage) is because it can be executed in many different ways. Other throws are less popular (such as deashiharai, kouchigari) because they can sustain only a few modifications and still remain effective. It is why trying to put them all in a text book is so difficult, to include all the variations is impossible, and to show only one standard form is misleading. Therefore, I have tried to refer to principles rather than to specifics. Here are some more principles relating to throws:

1. *Push* the opponent over the obstacle (leg, hip, body, etc.) you have put in his way. Do not *pull* him over it.

2. Get the driving leg outside the foot base.

3. Throw in a direction at right angles to the inside edge of the driving foot.

4. Keep your hands where you can see them.

5. Look to where you want to throw him.

6. When you are at the point of throwing him (kake), make sure you can *increase* the power and not lose it.

7. Make sure you can drive into

the direction of the throw and *not* fall out of it.

These are, of course, rule of thumb tips, so there will be plenty of exceptions, but on the whole they are sound words of advice for at least a starting point.

2. Counter-attacks

Again, there are far too many to be shown in a book of this kind, so let me make a few general points:

1. Any throw or grappling skill used as an offensive attack can be utilised as a defensive counter.

2. Countering attacks can be divided into two main sections:

(a) Early counters: just at the moment the opponent is about to launch his attack (the weakest moment), he is attacked (that's how the Israelis won the Six-Day War).

(b) Late counters: here the original attack has almost been successful, some effect has been achieved and the man is actually falling. However, as he falls he turns or twists and uses the force with which he is being thrown to throw the attacker.

3. Movement

This refers to the movement before and after the attacks, as well as that during them. Again, only generalities can be given here, but it should be remembered that movement, its quality and the control of it, is more important than

technique. Good movement control can always compensate for bad techique, whereas no technique, however 'good', can work if it is done with unco-ordinated movement.

1. The type of movement must reflect the personality of the performer.

2. The attacking movement must begin a few seconds before the technique starts.

3. The attacking movement must stop *after*, and not before, the opponent hits the floor or succumbs to a grappling technique.

4. The attacker's body must be 'in balance' throughout the whole action; there must be a harmonious flow from before the start to after the finish.

5. The pace of the movement must fit the action of the technique. Pace here refers to the movement *before* the attacking movement begins. The attacking movement is always as fast as circumstances allow; the pace of the movement is decided by the attack to be used. A rough guide is:

(a) ankle trips at a fast pace;

(b) one-legged throws, e.g. haraigoshi, osotogari, at a medium pace;

(c) two-legged throws, e.g. ipponseoi, taiotoshi, at a slow pace.

Again, it will depend precisely

upon how the throw is executed or modified as to which actual pace group it is in. A taiotoshi with no body contact can be done at a fast pace.

In groundwork arm locks are executed at a fast pace, strangles at a medium pace, and pins at a slow speed.

When it comes to building linked attacks (see next chapter) the pace of each attack is critical. One of the main purposes of a first attack is to change the opponent's pace in order to facilitate the next attack.

Some General Remarks

Talking about movement raises the whole problem of how to assess and analyse it. Movement is the essence of what most coaches' jobs are all about, yet surprisingly little time is devoted to it—in terms of analysis—by coaches. Movement is all about pace, rhythm, cadence, quality and patterns, which add up to an aesthetic value that can be attractive or disagreeable. A good coach will appreciate these qualities as part of many years' intimate knowledge of the sport, but he might not be able to express them in terms of the role they play in his coaching. He may use an aesthetic judgement when he is assessing the effectiveness of a certain skill, but yet not 'know' that he is doing so. To judge movement takes time; a study of anything related is valuable.

The camera has done much to destroy this ability to analyse movement. Because of the brilliant technological development of kinetography, plus the implicit cultural influence of classic Greek art in the 'freezing' of movement into rigid poses, the *still* has become the basis of contemporary movement study. Yet the still has been deprived of everything that movement is, i.e. rhythm and grace; how can it, then, be used to study *movement*?

The camera has committed another venal sin that has obfuscated the development of movement appreciation. Few have recognised or appreciated the weakness of the fixed viewpoint. Since the camera has a fixed location and only one eye, it makes a very 'irrational' picture taken from a single viewpoint. Convention has now accepted this as the only way to see a 'view' being looked at. It is conventionality reinforced by, for example, Renaissance painters who through their art implied that a panorama could only be seen from one fixed point in space. It is not true, of course. We are continually moving our heads and, with the slightest provocation, we move to another point of observation, so we can have an all-round, three-dimensional view of what we are looking at. The coach would not dream of standing still when he analyses an actual skill, and

therefore should not accept the camera's limited view of the truth.

Oriental painters have no affinity with this peculiar need to have a fixed viewpoint. Japanese artists, such as Okada Hanko and Tani Buncho, change it within their pictures several times to get a comprehensive view of a landscape, real or imaginary. Even in the West around the turn of the century there was a revolt against the conventionality towards movement and fixed viewpoints. Inspired by the work of such men as Mourey and Seurat, the Futurists in particular made an attack on the, by then, painting clichés. Pictures such as 'Red Horseman' by Carra and 'The Charge of Lancers' by Boccioni are well worth looking at to see the difficulties of representing *movement* in a two-dimensional frame. These artists clearly saw the problem, even if they did not find the answers.

> Cinematography does not trace the shape of movement. It subdivides it, without rules, with mechanical arbitrariness, disintegrating and shattering it without any kind of aesthetic concern for rhythm. It is not within its coldly mechanical power to satisfy such concerns ... We [the artists] are involved only in the area of movement which produces sensation, the memory of which still palpates in our awareness. We despise the

precise, mechanical, glacial reproduction of reality and take the utmost care to avoid it. For us this is a harmful and negative element, whereas for cinematography and chrisotography it is the very essence. (Anton Brogaglia, 1911.)

The date may be surprising, considering the contemporaneity of the expression, but those past artists' attitude could be that of the coach today. How does the coach analyse movement without destroying it in the process? There is a little research being done in this area, but not much. The camera has created the illusion that all the problems of analysing movement have been solved—by the camera. Perhaps some day science and art will co-operate to shed more light on this fascinating subject.

What's in a Name?

By now it may have occurred to the reader how important the technical terms are that are bandied around when judo is being taught. Words obviously not only transport meaning but are also symbols for actions. In both respects words can be misinterpreted and can cause much confusion. This has certainly happened in judo.

What often happens is that two forms (of a throw) have the same name, but their differences are forgotten. For example, two totally different forms of taiotoshi are taught as if they are the same. Japanese terminology, sometimes on purpose, but generally through ignorance, dictates and obscures what a judo skill is all about. Words like tsukuri, kuzushi, kake and randori are left to exert their own pernicious influence on skill teaching. The instructors cannot be bothered to insist on some kind of rational meaning; they are content to perpetuate the confusion of the past. Terminology should be used to clarify thought, not to suppress it. For example, the 'symbol' attached to tsukuri is of a man perched on one set of toes like a frozen ballerina. In this precarious position it is said he can easily be thrown. Of course he can—it is a self-evident truth. Kano used the illustration of the opponent standing on one set of toes, not to show how easily he could be thrown, but to indicate that his power is in proportion to the feet area which is in contact with the ground. Perched on one set of toes he has no power; standing on both feet he has a great deal of power.

Such ridiculous imagery has become so powerful over the generations that many fighters have a subliminal feeling that unless they get their opponents into this impossible position they are unable to throw them. Tsukuri has come to mean that impossible image, which is most unfortunate. It has blighted many young men's

fighting development. If the meaning of tsukuri were said simply to be preparation to attack, how much easier and more truthful it would be: it would help stimulate all kinds of preparations to attack. Naming techniques or skills should be done after the event and not before. When a throw is executed and, for some reason, a name is needed, call it something; exactly what is really immaterial, since it is a mere convenience. To use a name before the action only limits a performer's ability and hence breeds inadequacy.

There are times, of course, when a name is required to provide common ground between, for example, two coaches who wish to discuss some developing action. A name like taiotoshi may do the trick, but even then there are many dangers, for the name may be merely a symbol of each coach's personal attitude to performance. Both say 'Taiotoshi', but one means an attack against an inferior (skilled) opponent, while the other is referring to a physically weaker opponent. Not only does that mean the coaches see different structures in the biomechanical performances but also in the psychological attitude in the two attacks. So, although they are talking about the 'same' throw, i.e. taiotoshi, all aspects are quite different. In short, terminology must be used with great care.

THINKING

Thinking is probably something that goes on in the mind. What constitutes the mind is beyond comprehension. In the business of acquiring a physical skill we have to make a working guess at what thinking means because how we conceive it and how we believe it relates to the mind and has a bearing on how we teach skills.

When I was an up-and-coming fighter I was frequently told that if I saw an opening for an attack, I had already missed it. The explanation was that by the time the message (of seeing the opening) had gone up to my brain (mind?), been translated into other messages and sent back for initiation of action, it would be all too late. It seemed to have a touch of rationality about it. All I had to do was to throw 'without thinking'; I had to practise/repeat a throwing action so often that I could do it without thinking. Again, it sounded reasonable enough. The only snag was that when I tried to put this advice into practice (which I did for quite some time) I always used to get slammed on my ear.

I soon abandoned this approach to action and decided I had better think my way through everything I did. From then on I noticed a definite improvement.

What happens in practice, of course, is that thinking gets

confused with mental verbalisation. For about several thousand years we have been reading books and to do that we talk inside our heads, which we have come to accept as thinking.

I do not believe that; thinking is something different. Thinking is probably some kind of process that goes on in the mind. It used to be assumed that the mind was the water inside the sponge—the brain —but recently when doctors have been exploring the concept and practice of the brain bisection theory (i.e. the brain is in two parts which have an enigmatic but tenuous physical relationship between them) they have found that such a model does not relate to what happens in practice. The mind seems to be in different parts of the body, ready to respond immediately to any local need to act or react. Indeed, does even the skin limit the mind? How does the person with an amputated leg feel pain in his non-existing toes? How does the highly trained fighter know there is someone behind him? Is it the mind or is it thought? I like to believe it is thought—the dynamic process of the mind. Thinking goes on both inside and outside the body, yet at the same time it is a part of the mind, which in turn is a part of the body's physiology. As soon as action is needed, it happens, because thinking, like a fast reacting

28 Taiotoshi
(a) *White is ready to attack. He thrusts his right leg forwards, only a quarter turn.*

(b) *White drives Black backwards over the right leg; Black rolls round.*

computer, has registered the opportunity and moved the body at the same time. The essence of training is to get the thinking processes to recognise the needs of success.

When introducing the novice to new skills, the immediate purpose is not to introduce him to the technicalities of the action—where to put his hands and feet—but to how to recognise certain situations that will require a certain type of throwing skill. Let me give a few examples of how this could work in a learning situation, which might make the imponderable a little less daunting.

(c) *Once Black is in the air, White brings him round so that he lands in front of White.*

29 *Same start as taitoshi, but with a different end*

(a) White has 'missed' Black's right leg, and finds his right leg in between Black's legs.

(b) White can adjust quickly by hooking Black's left leg and throwing him backwards, or ...

(c) he can adjust slightly differently and throw Black forwards.

A Simple Approach

Let the two novices stand holding each other's jackets in the standard format. See photograph 28(a). Decide who is to throw and who is to be thrown. Let the thrown person move his right foot forwards, then back, forwards and back. He should allow his body weight to move with it. As the right foot moves back, the thrower steps and drives his right leg across the other man's legs and pushes him backwards over that blocking right leg. As the man falls over, the thrower turns him in the air so that he lands in front of the attacker. See photograph 28(c). The throw can now be called taiotoshi. If the attacker cannot reach the opponent's right leg, but only the left leg, he could do ouchigake, see photographs 29(a) and (b). It is not the intent that decides the name, but the effect.

A Complex Approach

Have the two move around the mats freely. However, get the man who is to be thrown to emphasise the backward movement of his right foot/leg. Tell the thrower that when he is ready he is to step forwards across the legs of the opponent and to push him back and then round that blocking right leg (see photograph 28(b)). Again, if successful it can be called taiotoshi; if the space between the bodies is too great, then uchimata can be done, see photographs 29(a) and (c).

Another Situation

Again, let the two novices stand still, holding each other's jacket in the standard way. This time tell Black to move his left foot/leg forwards and backwards, remembering to let the body weight move with it. As the left foot moves forwards, White steps slightly to the side and hooks his right leg in behind the left leg. He can now throw Black backwards (see photograph 29(b)), in which case it can be called ouchigake, or forwards, in which case it can be called uchimata (29(c)).

As with the other complex version, let the couple move around. This time Black emphasises the forward movement of his left foot/leg. When White is ready, he skips into position and hooks the right leg in and throws in whichever direction he feels is right.

Comments When the general movement pattern has been learned, the coach can begin to be specific about his instruction; pull with the left hand, push with the right, hook the leg in, keep the feet on the ground. These improvements will then be done in a moving pattern. The thrower can only learn the skill of throwing if the opponent provides the right circumstances. The circumstances dictate the throw. These circumstances will need to be given by the coach.

A TYPICAL LESSON PLAN

Let's assume the purpose of the coaching lesson is to develop the understanding of how to throw standing on one leg. (Any lesson should have a stated theme.)

Warm up In addition to the normal extension-type flexibility exercises, differing types of hopping exercises can be introduced. For example, cross the arms on the chest and hop around, gently banging into each other. This will introduce the idea of hopping and catching a body weight that is momentarily out of control.

Starting the Coaching

First, show what the man has to do, i.e. what are the right throwing circumstances he has to look for? He must move around quite fast and keep, in the main, his legs apart. This does not mean they should be held rigidly apart, or even apart all the time (they can even be crossed); it simply means that more often than not the legs will be making a broad base.

The total body shape must be held firmly in an upright posture. Everyone can practise that type of movement first of all. The coach will watch and help all to do it properly. The thrower must then be told what to look for in particular. Should he go for the opponent's nearest or farthest leg? By and large, it will be easiest to go for the nearest leg. He and the others can try hopping on their left legs. With any luck, various people will try to throw in different directions —some backwards, some forwards, some sideways.

The coach will stop each pair and help them with their version of solving the problem of how to throw in these circumstances.

He can then halt the activity and divide the class into small groups, with each sub-group consisting of pairs that are trying to do much the same thing. While he is looking after one group, improving their throwing skill, the other sub-groups can be doing groundwork. As members of each pair get to know what they have to do, they can move away and practise that. The coach can then work with the next sub-group and do much the same thing, but still keep an eye on the first.

The process is repeated, until all are coached. The number of coaches needed to handle all the sub-groups will depend largely on the size of the total group.

When a certain facility has been achieved partners could be changed. Remember: partners should not be changed too soon, as the change can cause much confusion. When partners change, skills change. How these alterations are caused and how they can modify the previous attack must be shown to each individual so that he can understand them. This process can be repeated till everyone has had experience of working with everyone else. By the end of a session each person should have 'felt' several similar throws performed in different ways.

Interspaced between this type of coaching could be groundwork sessions, *starting* from one of the many throwing situations experienced earlier. Remember, whenever possible there should be no dividing lines between throwing attacks and grappling attacks. They should flow in and out of the other as part of a total skill.

Now perhaps is the time to introduce the discussion period. A participant at any level should understand why and how he is doing what he is doing. The coach should explain the ideas behind the coaching and then encourage the group to discuss them with him. The coach could expand on some of the basic principles involved, and use them as a basis for discussion. For example:

1. When in a position to throw make sure you can *increase*, not lose, the power.

2. Do not expect your opponent to come to you; you should go to him.

3. Speed is for surprise; power is for consistency.

4. A contest skill is more important than scoring skills.

Relate these to the coaching that has already taken place. Try to get the group to relate these principles to the other tasks they are doing in training. The more they understand what is supposed to be happening, the quicker progress will be.

Now they have had a rest as well as a think, finish off the coaching session.

Use the same starting point in the second part of the session as in the first, i.e. group members to stand on one leg, but now to use the stance in the learning of counter-throwing. Counter-throws from this position are usually of the 'early' variety (see page 60), when little power is needed. Just as the opponent is about to attack, he is himself attacked with a fast throwing action. Throws such as harai tsurikomiashi, osotogari and haraigoshi are very effective in such circumstances. Again, explain what ought to be happening so that this can be used as a target at which to aim.

The session can be concluded with a short period of randori, but the group should be concentrating on the various aspects they have experienced in the session. It is not a time to play mindlessly, but to think, all the time, about what should be done.

The coach should be moving around continuously, trying to help solve difficulties as soon as they appear. Bad habits must not be allowed to form and become a part of the general movement. They must be rooted out, as quickly as possible. This is why the coach should always be on hand, watching.

Skill improvement is a matter of personal interaction between coach and performer. Both have to work at it; both have to help each other. Judo is such a complex business that neither side can afford to ignore the other.

3 THE END

The tension in the match has now imperceptibly changed again. The weight has moved back from the toes to the heels; offence has subtly changed to defence; great care has permeated the fighting atmosphere. Both men have had narrow escapes and both are glad still to be 'alive'. There are big changes in nervous tension as the hopes of winning and fear of losing rock backwards and forwards through their bodies. No longer is either prepared to charge into any opportunity offered: aggressive attack on demand is replaced with cautious probing. Fighting is always a gambling matter: the odds must be weighed, strengths and weaknesses assessed, decisions made, action launched. However, now exhaustion makes such gambles much less attractive. A hesitant attack will provoke a powerful and desperate counter-attack. In such conditions the advantage always lies with the defender, so who is going to risk an attack? It is a time when the encouragement of team-mates and coaches is needed. The fighters have got to be pushed over that sagging action line, for the first one to pull himself out of this state of fearful lethargy will probably win. Red Sash pulls his strength back through his fingers and toes and gets ready for the last great struggle. He tells himself forcibly what has got to be done. His powerful frontal attacks have still failed, although several did unnerve White Sash. He must use guile now: combinations, feints, dummy attacks. He must wrong-foot White. He must move how White Sash wants him to move, even if for only a second, for that will be enough. It may lull him into a false sense of security. He must at the same time tighten up his own attacks; one sloppy move now and all will be lost. He must keep both feet on the ground, whatever attack he uses, since that will make him very stable and hopefully strong at the moment he needs power and stability to terminate his attack. He feels mentally ready. He decides to try. He moves suddenly and unexpectedly to his right ...

SOME ATTITUDES TO THE END GAME

Does the end of a contest come after or before the beginning? This is not really an odd question. It depends upon the kind of end and beginning that is being talked about. Every contest is part of a chain of matches that runs through time. The past match influences the future match and, according to Hoyle, the future match influences the past. In *The Intelligent Universe* he writes: 'one must conclude, it seems to me, biological systems are able in some way to utilize the opposite time-sense in which radiation propagates from future to past. Bizarre as this may appear, they must somehow be working *backwards* in time'.

Knowledge is passed along the chain by experience and insight, and needs to be studied by those who want to win. Therefore, there is no beginning or end, other than in the referee's command; there is only a variation in the intensity of learning as represented by the fighting and non-fighting periods. Any coach appreciates the importance of non-fighting time in the total training session. It is the time of absorption, of reconciliation and of reconstruction, a time when nothingness teaches all those things that being cannot. Physical skills, such as judo skills, will shrivel and die if they are not regularly sustained by a liberal and frequent dose of the arts and sciences. A competitor with no appreciation of aesthetics is not so much an athletic philistine as what Spencer called 'a neo-barbarian'. To cultivate the body without doing the same for the mind is, to quote the Japanese, a way to produce a cripple. There are too many such cripples in judo today.

Life is, of course, a paradox. To talk in the above vein, however firmly believed, automatically introduces an incongruity which has handicapped judo for a long time. Dualism refers to the mind and the body, and it is so easy to slip into the habit of inferring that there are two separate entities—a mind and a body—which are to be treated separately.

Coaches are often heard making comments such as 'Ninety per cent of the action comes from the mind'. This statement would seem to be nonsensical, since quite obviously the action *is* in the body-work. However, at the same time we know what they are trying to say. They mean that if the mind is not entirely absorbed into the action, then the action is bound to be inefficient, but the coaches have great difficulty in taking the next thinking step in this process of reconciliation: the mind is the body and the body is the mind. To train one is to train the other. That is why, if the skill is to be a combination of science and art (which it must be), then training must contain both scientific and artistic elements. At the very height of a heavy training programme my judo teacher would take me off to a concert, an art gallery or a theatre. How many training programmes contain that kind of training in the non-fighting time?

As knowledge of physiology increases, the medical fraternity has to concede it has greater and greater difficulty in distinguishing where the 'body' stops and the 'mind' begins. When it comes to fast action that part of the body nearest the movement may 'think' on its own and may not be controlled by the brain. Such independent thinking could mean that emergency action may be initiated locally and not by the brain. That could speed things up considerably!

Certainly, there are aspects of highly developed physical skills which border on the mystical. If the training has been of high quality a throw, for example, can be performed 'without doing'. It means the throw is executed without the thrower apparently knowing he has done it; the opponent just flies in a marvellously effortless way. The Japanese use the word mushin in such an instance, meaning not so much that there is no 'thinking' but rather because there is no interference between external and internal elements, such as thinking about how mind is to be co-ordinated with action.

Of course, the mind works in ways we cannot begin to understand. Just as soon as one philosopher works out a new model to explain an unknown function, another inexplicable function immediately takes its place.

In an 'eyeball to eyeball' competitive skill like judo these mystical aspects of performance are highlighted. When the fighter is fresh, is full of vitality and possesses an exuberance to do more than he is actually capable of, he has no consideration for the body/mind problem. He takes it fully for granted that he will function as a totally co-ordinated organism, in complete harmony with himself, the opposition and the environment. When he is tired, however, this harmony tends to disintegrate. The major elements—himself, the opponent, the situation—become disassociated and one of them, usually the opponent, moves out of perspective and destroys the harmony and hence the skill. What can the competitor do to hold the harmony?

The 'no mind' state is the one in which every champion wants to be; the mind is not attached to any single point of the combined body mass. It does not focus on the opponent's feet, face or body, but encloses the whole competitive unit (e.g. the two fighters, referee, judge and spectator). To achieve this the fighter must have trained, the most direct way being through meditation and preferably using a system that has had a long history and tradition on which to depend and is therefore one that has experience of the dangers as well as of the advantages of meditation (e.g. Zen).

Here is not the place to expand on this subject. Under stress, power, or energy, seems to run out through the fingers and toes and somehow the fighter has got to be able to pull it back through those exits and hold it in the centre of his body (in Japanese it is called the saikatanden), ready to be used when and wherever needed.

ABOUT WINNING AND LOSING

How does the fighter lose? How can the contest end? The answer to such questions always lies in the rules (the implementation of the answers is the responsibility of the fighter), so let's look at the rules:

End of Contest (*Article 20*)
The referee shall announce 'soremade' (that is all) and end the contest:

(a) When one contestant scores ippon or waza-ari awasete ippon (Articles 21 and 22).

(b) In the case of sogo-gachi (compound win) (Article 23).

(c) In the case of fusen-gachi (win by default) or kiken-gachi (win by withdrawal) (Article 30).

(d) In the case of hansoku-make (disqualification) (Article 29).

(e) When one contestant cannot continue due to injury (Article 31).

(f) When the time allotted to the contest has expired (see hantei).

Upon the announcement of soremade by the referee, the contestants shall return to their starting positions.

It is a much more complicated business to stop the match than to start it!

Start of Contest (*Article 16*)
Before the start of each contest, the three officials (referee and two judges) shall stand together inside the limits of the competition area (and centred) and shall bow before taking their places.

The contestants shall stand facing each other on the contest area at the assigned red or white tape corresponding to the sash they are wearing. After the contestants have made the standing bow and taken one step forward, the referee shall announce 'hajime' to start the contest.

The contest shall always begin in the standing position.

This is quite straightforward (although I am not really sure how a contest stands up!) To study the ways of ending a match can certainly be useful when building a training programme. For example: Hansoku is the breaking of the rules, particularly with reference to Article 28. There are 12 sub-sections to this article and the aspiring competitor must know them all—thoroughly! There are two levels of punishment the referee can impose, depending on the blatancy of the foul. The competitor must know how these assessments are made and how they are applied. It is a disgrace to lose by Hansoku (unless it is completely outside the control of the competitor, e.g. the referee makes a gross error). The competitor needs to understand what a sogo win means in terms of his performance. If the opponent has been penalised by a keikoku (see Article 28) he only needs to score waza-ari for a terminal score win.

That will need practice.

Injury is normally something that happens in an unforeseen circumstance and therefore cannot be avoided. However, there are two things that can be done in training which can minimise these material risks:

1. Use support bandaging on high risk joints (e.g. knees, elbows, shoulders, ankles) before they are injured. Avoidance is always better than cure. In my youth it was considered cowardly to wrap up in this way, but we did suffer for our foolhardy bravery. Many were left with life-long injuries because they would not wrap up *after* the injury, let alone before it!

2. Train to be flexible: anticipate dangerous situations. Many injuries are caused by competitors stiffening in defence, trying to stave off an attack by hardness of the body. Such rigidity is frequently broken and, in the process, the body gets broken, too. Train to move away from an attack; keep the body soft but strong. Close the body spaces when defending; do not open them.

Finally, two wazaaris can win a contest. Ippons and wazaaris are

the most economical way of winning a match. Energy and power are saved for later contests and, more importantly, the big scores frighten future opposition. An ippon is almost as valuable in the last phase of a contest as it would be in the first. The future opposition will think you can do it any time—at the end or the beginning—and that's good psychological warfare.

Is the tired skill the same as a fresh skill? Of course not; any fighter will tell you that. The inexperienced fighter who has, say, an uchimata that he always uses will try to utilise it at the end of a contest in the same way as at the start. No wonder he gets countered—the 'bounce' in the movement will be missing, the rhythm will be wrong and the co-ordination will be just that touch too slack. When fresh,

30 A tired ouchi

(a) *(top) White attacks with ouchi, but because he is tired he has allowed Black's head to stay up (see photograph 30(a)); he has also left his left leg too far to the side.*

(b) *With the use of his head Black Swings his right shoulder forwards and then uses his left foot to kick White's left foot out from under him.*

the mind can be everywhere: as meditation will have taught, the fresh mind will encompass the whole body. When the body is tired, the whole skill disintegrates and the parts slide away out of control. The badly trained fighter tries to chase these parts and in the process loses his grip on the entire match. During training the coach will have recorded the strengths and weaknesses of every member of his squad. The individual must learn what his particular weaknesses and strengths are and how they vary when he is fresh and when tired. He will then be able to recognise them in competition and so control them. Too often the champion loses through his strong points, because he unnecessarily takes too much care of his weak ones. The exploitation of the strong points protects the weak ones. Training must correct such a wrong emphasis.

EXAMPLES OF TIRED SKILLS

When doing a 'fresh' uchimata, it is essential that the opponent's right sleeve arm is pulled in tight. This brings the right shoulder forwards, making countering difficult (just as it makes throwing easy). When tired, this tightness is often allowed to slacken, very slightly; the opponent pulls his right shoulder back—and the attacker is 'flying'!

When attacking with a tired ouchi, the major push tends to be put on the opponent's *left* shoulder. The body is allowed to hollow out too much and it becomes easy for the opponent to twist and counter-throw to his left (see photographs 30(a) and (b)).

The effectiveness of newaza skills can be greatly eroded by tiredness. What begins as a powerful osaekomi, within ten seconds can become a nightmare, like hanging on a cliff with just the finger tips hooked into a crack in the rock face. The choice about what to do can be just as horrible: to hang on may mean you get turned over easily and then find yourself in a pin, but to let go and try to regain the vertical may present the opponent with a great opportunity for an attack and you will not have the strength to block it. Whether throwing or grappling when tired, the part must become the whole and must fill the moment. If a pin is being attempted, the most important factors must be understood and they must be the focus of power. The opponent's head must be tightly controlled (see photograph 31). The attacker must put all his concentration on that point. At the start of the match there may well be lots of movement by the attacker, each move blocking the opponent's attempt to escape and all helping to tire the opponent out. At the end of the match the attacker will be trying to stay still, conserving his energy and clamping hard the opponent's head.

It is, of course, very difficult to make specific points about this matter of tiredness affecting skills. Every individual will be affected in totally different ways. One man's legs may solidify so that he cannot move them when the attack is made; another's hands will fail (his fingers will not hold) and he will not be able to pull a cork out of a

*31 **Kuzurekami shiho gatame***
Notice how Black's head is 'jammed' between White's body and left elbow, and how White keeps his head up to keep pressure on Black and facilitate manoeuvrability.

32 (a) **A fighting ipponseoinage.** Notice how the attacker's left leg is behind his right, and the opponent has been rolled across the attacker's back.

32 (b) **A fighting taiotoshi.** There are almost as many ways of doing taiotoshi as there are people doing it!

bottle; another will not be able to stabilise his hip area and when he attacks he will break in the middle like a dried straw. These feelings must be known and experienced, and included in the individual's training programme.

When they appear in competition the man must be able to recognise them and then know what to do about them.

Here are some principles to remember when tired.

1. Avoid using techniques that demand standing on one leg, e.g. haraigoshi, osotogari, deashiharai.

2. Use only those that involve having both feet on the ground (at kake). If they do not normally require both feet to be on the ground (e.g. uchimata), then modify them so that both feet *are* on the ground at kake (see photographs 29(a)—(c)).

3. Movement will be sluggish, so do not use attacks that need fast reactions, e.g. sutemiwaza. Use throwing actions that can 'absorb' many mistakes, without losing *all* effectiveness, e.g. ipponseoinage, taiotoshi (see photographs 32(a) and (b)).

4. Know the rules: when tired and ippons have to be tried for, do them at the edge of the contest area. If things go wrong you can always accidentally slip over the edge.

5. Rest the eyes and lungs away from the fighting area. To watch too many fights (other than those of direct concern to you) is to encourage blurred perception and tiredness; the body then becomes sympathetically tired. Get some fresh air during the day's tournament. Go out for a short walk (wrap up warm if it is cold).

The air in a stadium full of people and fighting competitors can soon become stale; little oxygen and stagnant air are not good for a man who has to give maximum effort!

WHAT ABOUT TACTICS?

In the middle phase of the match (see the second chapter) tactics are concerned with the use of single skills: when and how to do uchimata in different kinds of situations; what kind of conditions are needed for a pin or a strangle? It is the time of the big battalions when different kinds of force are used in the most effective manner (see page 78). However, as we have already discovered, at the outset of this last phase Red Sash has had no success with these direct attacks. Not only have they failed, but he has got very close to being countered. So, he decides to use cunning and guile, rather than overt force. In short, he decides he is going to use combination attacks (renrakuwaza) or linked attacks.

In a real contest, of course, a fighter may well decide to use linked attacks any time during the match, but here in this very special event with which we are involved, I am suggesting that such attacks are best used at the end (with some justification). There are many forms of linked attacks with a range of specific but different objectives to achieve, but all have

the ultimate purpose of winning. Without this tactics become a spiritless sequence of movements. So, let's see what are some of the objectives:

1. Change the conditions: this means alter the location of the fight within the contest area; change the shape of the opponent (straight, crouched, sideways stance, etc.); change the pace of the match (faster or slower); change the psychology of the opponent (destroy his readiness to attack or to defend).

2. Change the circumstances: in such a way that they will facilitate certain throws or ground skills. This type of objective may mean linking just two attacks or several (up to, say, seven or eight). The length of the sequence will depend to some degree on the conditions needed— does the opponent need to be confused or bewildered, or made more tired to inhibit his attack?

3. Change the style: this means produce unorthodoxy and loss of pattern (by the opponent). Usually when planning attacking sequences the best method will be to alternate types of throw, for example, a head roller or a body twister (see pages 43 and 44), but sometimes it is useful to link several rollers and then several twisters, or vice versa. Again, it is impossible to cover all these variations in a short

book of this kind, but let me try to give a couple of examples.

A Combination to Produce a Change of Body Shape and Pace

Number 1 The purpose is to allow an osotogake to be executed at the moment the opponent is moving slowly but standing straight. This first attack works best with a fast-moving, crouched opponent.

33 A tachiwaza combination

(a) They are moving around fast (notice Black is off the ground).

(b) White stabs out a 'feeble' taiotoshi.

(c) Black steps easily over White's right leg, but in doing so quickens the pace faster still.

(d) White attacks with sasai and Black steps over it, but Black quickly slows the pace right down — for fear of more foot trips.

(e) However, this is what White wants; he encourages Black to move slowly ...

White attacks hard, but with very little weight commitment, with taiotoshi. Black steps forwards easily and quickly over the extended leg (increasing the general pace of the match), see photograph 33(c). After waiting for one or two steps White makes a foot trip attack (sasai tsurikomiashi). Black blocks the attack by stopping and standing straight and stiff (he is tired), so that his feet do not slide. White hits him with osotogake.

(f) and he finishes with an osoto.

34 Newaza combination

(a) Black reaches and holds the back of White's collar, ready to roll him over.

(b) White grabs the left arm and starts to move.

(c) White swings right round.

(d) White pulls Black's left arm in tight to his chest.

(e) White begins to roll back, swinging his left leg across Black's body.

(f) The finished arm-lock.

Number 2 The purpose is to get a straight arm lock when both contestants are on the ground. White is on top of Black (see photographs 34(a) and (b)). To create an arm lock situation White must quicken the pace; at the moment Black is very defensive, lying on his side. White sacrifices his strong position (this is a calculated risk) by going for a strangle (photograph 34(a)) (not one from the front, for that would tie up his hands and would be much too dangerous). Black quickly brings his feet up and rolls fast to his right. He reaches up with his left arm; White grabs the arm and moves into the lock.

When you try these two simple combination attacks, what do you notice about them? Let me say what I think you should have appreciated:

1. The attacker must know what he is doing and must have the confidence to do it.

2. There must be a mental intent to complete the early attacks, even if there is no physical intent. Inexperienced fighters think they have to make physical contact with an attack if the opponent is to respond.

This is true for novices, but not for good class performers. They need only be *threatened* with a particular attack. Once the opponent feels the threat, he will respond.

3. The attacker must be able to change the sequence of attack, even after it has been started.

To discover more about tactics there is no better way than to read the battle plans of the great generals. It is surprising how similar the battles between hundreds of men are to that between two men.

Hannibal has already been mentioned; look also at Genghis Khan, Napoleon, Marlborough, Sun Tsu ... All that is needed is a 'transfer key phrase'. In battle tactics there are two basic terms, 'frontal' and 'flank' attacks; in judo tactics the equivalents are 'inside' and 'outside' attacks. 'Inside' refers to those attacks which happen between the opponent's arms (see figs 3(a) and 3(b)). 'Outside' refers to those made outside the opponent's arms. When a general talks about frontal attacks, the judo man says inside attacks; once that is accepted the rest is easy to translate from the military to the civilian.

Most generals do not like frontal attacks (and it is the only attack that traditional judo teaches!) It is too costly, and results in too many casualties (counters!) It is also too obvious. Napoleon would only consider a frontal attack if his centre massively outweighed the opposition's front and the flanks had been harassed sufficiently by cavalry and cannon. Even then he demanded great flexibility between his troops. They had to be able to change the weight of attack from right to left and back, quickly. There are few judo fighters who can attack from the flanks, on the outside. The 'spin turn' is, of course, a well established way of doing flank attacks (see photographs 35(a)—(f), but it has long been out of fashion. It is due for a revival!

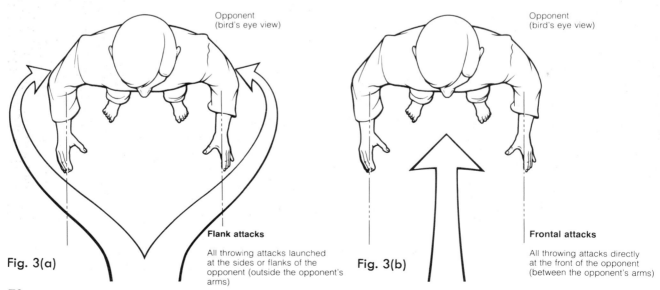

Opponent
(bird's eye view)

Opponent
(bird's eye view)

Flank attacks

All throwing attacks launched at the sides or flanks of the opponent (outside the opponent's arms)

Frontal attacks

All throwing attacks directly at the front of the opponent (between the opponent's arms)

Fig. 3(a)

Fig. 3(b)

35 A spin turn
(a) White starts the attack.

(b) White moves his right leg and then ...

(c) his left leg moves across.

(d) White spins on the left foot.

(e) White's right leg whips Black's legs out from under him.

(f) Again, the generated momentum takes White right over Black's body.

Since the Japanese terminology of judo philosophy is largely misunderstood in many areas, the use of force has been badly misrepresented when teaching judo skills. In judo circles, ju, the first ideograph of judo, is invariably translated as meaning 'soft', 'gentle', 'giving way', thus producing the meaning of judo in common use as 'the gentle way', 'the soft way'. This is a travesty of Kano's intention when he coined the name 'judo'.

Chinese philosophers have several simple concepts that weave in and out of their thinking, irrespective of whether the system is called Taoist, Buddhist or Confucian. The idea of opposites, of balance, of the yin and the yang, is one of those concepts. Life is sustained by the dynamic tension between opposites: beauty and ugliness, truth and lies; although yin is usually said to be the passive aspect and yang the active, the roles are not permanent. No one single principle or viewpoint can exist without an opposite. If there is a 'ju' there must be an opposite. In Japanese the ideograph is read as 'go'. Ju is the exploitation of weakness (thus making it one form of force), while go is the exploitation of strength (a different kind of force). In his writings, Kano refers many times to the importance of the interaction between ju and go and, what is

more, he formulated a kata on both principles. Most well informed judo people know about the ju-no-kata (although very few understand it), but unfortunately the go-no-kata has been lost. I have tried to fill this gap by devising one of my own. An individual who wishes to fight well —or live well—must know and use both principles in the most propitious way possible.

So, what is ju, in practical terms? Let me give an example. Both men are standing. White Sash is pushing hard, with both hands, into Red Sash's chest. Red holds himself against the push, not giving way. White pushes harder. Red still does not give way but braces strongly against the push. Suddenly Red Sash gives way (like a dam breaking under great water pressure). White Sash momentarily lurches forwards. Red turns, drops slightly and swings in for an uchi-mata.

Notice the pattern: a force (push) is contained. Then, when its strength has been assessed, it is unblocked and allowed to move; the push is now reinforced by the counter-attacker's force and used to throw the pusher. It should be realised that this is not a pattern of weakness but of strength, strength added to strength.

What is go? There is the same force, the push. It is contained and

then, when its strength has been assessed, a greater force is used to drive it back from where it has come; i.e. strength overcomes strength.

Both men are standing. White Sash pushes hard into Red Sash's chest. Red holds the push, then suddenly drives hard, right through the push, and attacks with osoto.

Here, too, the pattern is one of strength. Weakness without strength has little value in a fighter's life style.

As Kano writes, judo competition is a conflict of control: it is about who can control the various uses of power best. Tactics are the plan to implement a chosen form of control. Sometimes it lasts only a few seconds, while at other times it is for the duration of the whole contest.

The coach, watching every contest his competitors are in, will record their changing and developing patterns of strengths and weaknesses. He will produce them at subsequent training sessions and will build improving methods into the individual's training plan. No two training sessions will be the same; perhaps there will be a consistency in the heading of a section, e.g. Skill Improvement, but for the individual every training stint will be (and must be) different.

In the past, judo training sessions were all the same; first there was some irrelevant to performance 'warm up' and then some irrelevant static exercise (called uchikomi), followed by randori, when everybody did just what they liked. No care was taken of the individual at all. No single person was expected to discuss his strengths and weaknesses; no one was expected to know what he was supposed to be doing. Nobody did know what they were doing! For Kano, training was a form of education, meaning that the individual had to know what he was doing and comprehend why he was doing it.

Back in the 1890s in Japan, Japanese youth were being battered by the culture shocks between east and west. They were losing their social orientation and hence losing all kinds of behavioural standards. Kano, along with many other educationalists of the time, realised they had to be buttressed against this buffeting and to be provided with living ethical standards of behaviour. Kano saw judo, among other forms of physical education, as a means of providing standards of moral conduct for the youth to learn, experience and utilise.

Kano divided his training plan into three parts. All were designed to improve skill within a moral framework. They were called kata, randori and shiai. They contained elements of obligation, rights, responsibilities and competition, as well as a means of improving skill, but in differing degrees of emphasis.

KATA

Kata roughly means 'form'.

For Kano the most important part of training was kata. It is a structured series of movements, to improve skill, constrained by time and purpose. There is a beginning and an end (just like shiai) and between those 'bookends' of start and stop are designed movement patterns that will illustrate certain skill principles and, when experienced, will improve that skill.

Space in this book is too limited to go into any depth regarding the scope of kata, but two disparate forms will be briefly described so that the reader can obtain some idea of what they demand.

Nage-no-kata (the form of throwing)

This sequence was devised and refined by Kano over a period of something like ten years. It attempts to show various throwing actions in relation to certain physical criteria. There was much trial and error, with different throws being tried in a fixed sequence of fifteen throws. The title, 'the form of throwing', implies that all types of throwing actions should be included, but this is not the case and only a few types have been chosen. They are looked at from a biomechanical point of view: how are the hands, hips, legs and body weight used? It is a very simplistic approach to the analysis of throwing skills and therefore suffers much from that superficiality. However, in many ways it is a useful introduction to the study of throwing, if the person in charge does understand the strengths and weaknesses of kata performance.

Itsutsunokata (the form of 'five')

It was the last kata Kano structured. Like many other creative men, his practical work tended to become more abstracted as he grew older, although as Picasso said 'nothing at all abstract, as everything has to start from reality'. This kata attempts to isolate and demonstrate the five main principles underlying life itself. It is an example of the Victorian aspiration to explain the inexplicable in one very simple 'law' or in general 'rules'.

In the order of the kata they are:

1. Direct force: the 'attacker' moves directly at the 'opponent' and overcomes him with superior strength (go).

2. Exploitation of force: the 'attacker' moves directly at the 'opponent' who avoids it and uses it for his own purpose (ju).

3. Interactive force: both protagonists direct their respective forces at one another; the forces meet, interact, and then fly off in new, different directions.

4. Indirect force: the 'attacker' adopts a circuitous route, so that he strikes the 'opponent' from an unexpected direction. As a result he easily overcomes the 'opponent'.

5. Negation of force: the 'attacker' moves directly at the 'opponent'; the 'opponent' avoids the force totally, thus causing the force to whirl away out of control.

The intent, and the structure, is certainly a very admirable one and no doubt its success will depend upon the scepticism of the performer, but there is always the perennial response, 'Could you do better?' Of course, every conscientious coach will not only study all traditional kata assiduously, but will make up his own for his own purposes. For example, when the coach teaches a particular combination attack he is teaching a kata of that attack. Here are a couple of standard combination kata:

Ouchigake linked to taiotoshi The ouchi is made at speed and is only a threat, see photographs 36(b) and (c). The opponent reacts very slightly by adjusting his weight away from the leg that is attacked/threatened to the other

36 **Ouchi changed to taiotoshi**
(a) White is ready to attack.

(d) White drops into taiotoshi ...

(b) White jumps: not so much that his shoulders raise — he just tucks his legs up.

(c) The camera motor drive is not fast enough to catch the touch by White's right foot of Black's inside left leg. Immediately, on the reaction of Black ...

(e) White drops into taiotoshi ...

(a)

(b)

(c)

(d)

84

(e)

leg. That is enough; the attacker drops and finishes the movement with taoiotoshi and scores.

Sasai tsurikomiashi linked to osotogake The sasai is made very strongly to the opponent's left side; to avoid it he steps over the blocking foot with his left foot. The attacker keeps pulling with his right hand, see photographs 37(a)—(e), and the opponent finds he has to move forwards several steps, but being careful he slows the movement down. As he does so, the attacker goes in hard for a right-sided osotogake.

To practise such sequences is, in effect, performing kata.

37 *Sasai converted to osoto*

(a) White is ready; he brings his left foot towards his right to facilitate the touching of Black's left foot with his right foot. Again, the camera has missed the shot as the move is so fast.

(b) Black reacts against the move to his left. White puts his right foot to the floor and begins to move towards Black's right side.

(c) White's left foot moves sideways, allowing White to get his hips behind the swinging right leg.

(d) White finishes the attack.

RANDORI (FREEPLAY)

This is a very unstructured form of training. The trainees are expected to experiment with their skills in order to improve them. It is, of course, competitive and can therefore be violent. The limit of that violence is set by the consideration of each man for the other. It was here that Kano saw the importance of moral training. Each man must learn to respect the other; to recognise weaknesses, but not to take advantage of them; to appreciate lack of skill and to help eradicate, rather than exploit, inadequacy.

Too often this aspect of training is forgotten and randori is used as a means of beating up the inexperienced and the unskilful. It is a pity, because without a doubt the major factor in randori should be the inculcation of a moral code of behaviour. Any skill improvement is merely a bonus to that purpose. Some coaches try to suggest that randori is just a skill improvement exercise and that it is the only way to improve. This is a gross exaggeration: randori is an extremely poor way of improving skill. (Look at the time it takes for improvement in those who only take part in randori.) The participants seldom repeat the skill (a kind of repetition is an essential element in skill improvement) and never study the circumstances of the skill. Finally, the main fault is that it teaches students only how to fail!

SHIAI (COMPETITION)

Here the trainees are testing their skills, and discovering if and how they have improved (or degenerated!) Unlike randori there are time constraints and imposed rules of performance; there is usually a winner and a referee is needed to decide who that winner is.

A code of ethics is very much demanded of the competitors, as outlined in the rules and dictated by social expectations. The skill performance is greatly restricted by the rules, time and obligations between performers. All that creates great stress on the participants and the test is: can they still do the skills they have learned in kata?

SKILL ACQUISITION

How is skill acquired? In the first chapter at the start of the contest I talked about skill being technique absorbed by the individual and then interacting with an ephemeral set of circumstances. If the interaction is positive there is success; if it is negative there is failure. At the end of the match, in this chapter, skill has been presented as being concerned with holding the 'strings' together, rallying all the forces together to regain the standard of performance lost through fatigue. Yet the paradox is that even if everything is pulled together successfully, it will not be the same as the 'fresh skill' and, who knows, it may even be better! Even when skills are supposedly the same, they are, in actual fact, different.

You can never do the same skill twice. The coach will need to assess the personality of the performer so that he can mould a technique to fit him and him only. As the man wins and loses, so certain superficial aspects of his personality will change and that will mean his skills will have to be modified. Because he wins his first match with taiotoshi, it does not necessarily follow that he will win his last match with it. During a competitive career of, say, 5–7 years a man's fighting weight may increase by 20 or even 50 lb. That will almost certainly mean a change in technique and definitely a change of skill.

Any alteration the coach wants to make will have to be done through discussion with the performer and he must understand the reasoning behind it. Such close contact between coach and fighter usually means the coach only has enough time to look after a handful of performers. He will need to keep extensive records of each performer, monitoring closely each person's performance. If an individual begins to develop beyond the capability and experience of the coach, that coach must be prepared to pass him on to a more suitable coach if necessary.

Sometimes a coach is given a squad of 30 or 40 performers to look after. This means he cannot coach them, only train them. He shouts out certain numbers and they will respond like performing dogs, running and jumping accordingly. Such an approach does have its own advantages, but they have very little to do with skill acquisition. The other alternative is, of course, to have specialist coaches who are particularly good at linked attacks, tactics, power skills or other specific kata. Two or three squad members would be given to these specialists for a certain period of time and then moved on to another one. In this way every person would receive individual attention.

Let's try to summarise planning for competition.

1. It must be based upon the needs of the individual.

2. It must change its content regularly:

(a) to accommodate the changes in the individual, and

(b) to accommodate the changes in fighting styles (e.g. this year the emphasis in competition is on groundwork, next year on sutemiwaza, etc).

3. It must try to anticipate change, and to create new skills rather than to chase old ones.

4. Fitness and stamina training must be supplementary to skill training so they remain within the skill performance and do not dominate and thereby limit it.

5. Specialised skills, e.g. throwing and grappling, as well as tactical skills, e.g. how to fight a match, must be analysed and studied continuously so that their essential elements can be improved all the time.

6. The coach-competitor relationship is very important and numbers should be kept low—say, one coach to four or five trainees. In this way the coach will be able to provide the necessary support as technical adviser, tactical analyst and counsellor of matters indirectly connected with training.

7. The training for the end of the contest must be different from that for the beginning, and each must vary from training for the middle.

MOTIVATION

The influence of personality on skill has already been mentioned. If those classifications of personality called introversion and extroversion were accepted, then skills can be seen as being introverted and extroverted. Some competitors will develop skills that are very tight and contained, while others will produce skills that are very open and expansive. Motivation is another similar factor that will influence skill growth unnoticed by the near-sighted coach.

What is motivation? Is it a part of the personality? Is it innate or acquired? As with other nominalistic words, it depends on your prejudice. Contemporary thinkers on the subject seem to see motivation as an energy resource within the individual which fluctuates according to the exhortations of some fanatical enthusiast (called the coach). It can be that, of course, but too often such exhortation is only a way of covering up bad coaching and teaching. If the competitor is hyped up enough, he can forget how little he knows about how to fight the coming battle and so he can fight 'blind'.

Psychologists of the more recent past tended to see motivation as an innate drive, a need to achieve, an early form of Maslowism; motivation for them was a thrust towards some inner nebulous purpose.

McDougal, one of those early psychologists, described 'drive' as 'a propensity that is within an innate constitution that will generate an active tendency (talent) towards an ongoing goal'.

My own research would support such an approach. The need to take part in a particular kind of sport seems to materialise early, even before puberty, although it often remains intangible till the right opportunity offers itself. Many champions were taken to their sport, by parents or friends, seemingly by accident, yet as soon as they began playing they found it quite 'natural' and they stayed with it. This drive continues and sustains dedication until it succeeds or it is destroyed by such factors as no facilities, disapproval by the surrounding community, or bad coaching. The conscientious coach is aware of that; it is why he will study the individual and design the training programme for each individual. The great enemy of motivation is boredom.

Motivation of this innate kind, where progress is not so much anticipated as assumed, is not only paradoxical but difficult to comprehend—not by the people who have it, but by those who are expected to guide it. It produces a significant problem: should knowledge be 'pushed into' the individual or should it be allowed to 'come out'? An American psychologist said, 'You only learn what you already know'. The orient tends to take the view that psychic barriers have to be broken down (usually through meditation), thus allowing the skills to emerge in their own pristine glory, whereas the west tends to bang the information into the individual. However, this is changing, yet still the west has to have a rational explanation of motivation, on the basis that there must be some recognisable reason for people doing things (such as winning). Therefore, some psychologists have invented two explanations. There is extrinsic motivation, meaning the incentive is for 'external' recognition, e.g. medals, cups, prizes of all sorts, and there is intrinsic motivation, meaning that satisfaction, achievement and pleasure are the incentive. Of course, such explanations will cover many people, but not all; there is the poetic inexplicable, the doing simply because it must be done. The performer does not question why, he simply acts. The

conscientious coach will recognise that, too. The plan for each person will be unique. Such a plan may well not emphasise long-term objectives, but will provide short-term targets that the individual can modify to fit into his own long-term needs. Many painters show this indifference to 'organised growth'. Leonardo had great problems finishing the many paintings he started, because although they were his creations, they were still leading him where his 'instinct' did not want him to go. More recently Picasso, in 'The artist of the moment', writes vividly of his attitude to long-term objectives:

The several manners I have used in my art must not be considered as an evolution, or as steps toward an unknown ideal of painting. All I have ever made was made for the present and with the hope that it will always remain in the present. I have never taken into consideration the spirit of research. When I have found something to express, I have done it without thinking of the past or of the future. I do not believe I have used radically different elements in the different manners I have used in painting. If the subjects I have wanted to express have suggested different ways of expression I have never hesitated to adopt them. I have never made trials nor experiments. Whenever I had something to say, I have said it in the manner in which I have felt it ought to be said. Different motives inevitably require different methods of expression. This does not imply either evolution or progress, but an adaptation of the idea one wants to express and the means to express that idea.

In the old days pictures went forward toward completion by stages. Every day brought something new. A picture used to be a sum of additions. In my case a picture is a sum of destructions. I do a picture—then I destroy it. In the end, though, nothing is lost; the red I took away from one place turns up somewhere else.

The need to express is in the here and now and that is what is important. This innate drive to create spontaneously seems to have something to do with 'self-identification'. People need to be recognised as separate individuals. There is a horror of being totally anonymous, of being completely indistinguishable from all others. Writers like Kafka and Orwell have exploited these fears for their own artistic ends. To avoid this frightening anonymity people will try to create something of their very own by which they can be recognised and which is them. The degree or the magnitude of that creation will depend upon the size of their talent. Whatever the talent, it will need to interact with its environmental stimuli to become a creative skill. The result of that interaction may be just a knitted jumper or the 'last supper'; the artistic standard is immaterial—it demonstrates individuality. If there is no talent at all (hardly believable), or if the talent fails to find the right stimulus to flower, then the individual is poor indeed. In this case he may need to resort to bizarre clothes, vandalism and drugs to show who he is, or to stop himself from recognising who he is. Skill in sport is an obvious way of achieving self-identification; the skill is easily identified and therefore so is the individual who performs it. In Japanese judo circles, if a man has a very common name like Suzuki (Smith would be the English equivalent), he would be singled out by his best throw, e.g. Taiotoshi Suzuki. Winning is sometimes merely an extension of that need to be recognised. The man is not necessarily interested in winning as such, but winning ensures him a place in the list of recognisable people. Judo people are very existential; they are what they are by doing what they do.

Sartre, somewhat unexpectedly, has a sound understanding of why a sportsman takes part in sport, i.e. 'to attain himself as a certain being, precisely the being which is in question in his being'. The 'question' obviously relates to his identification (who is he?). Such a 'search' can give an impression of 'lack of direction', for if the competitor is asked why he trains so hard, he may reply that he does not know (to say 'to find myself' would be just as ridiculous to him as to the listener). However, the coach should not take that 'know not' literally and start to berate him for his lack of purpose. Not knowing may be more profound than 'I want to win' or 'I want to be the best'. It could well generate a greater dedication to performance improvement than all the rest of the more mundane reasons put together. The coach must build that, too, into the individual's training programme.

SUMMARY

1. Finishing skills are different from starting skills.

2. The training programme must accommodate both starting and finishing skills.

3. There must be tactics, lasting for the whole of the contest or for only a part of it; the fighters must

understand these tactics and must be able to modify them, constructively, on the spot or during training.

4. Learn the rules: know what the scores mean in practical throwing and grappling circumstances.

5. Study and practise linked attacks (and counters). Remember the movement *between* the attacks is more important than the attacks themselves.

6. There are different kinds of strengths/power available to the fighter. He must learn to develop them and use them all.

7. Training is the time to learn ethical behaviour as well as competitive skills; competition without morality is group vandalism.

8. No two skilled performances are the same (even if they are the same throw or pin). Variations and why they change must be studied, and that is a never-ending process.

9. Boredom is the enemy of motivation.

10. The need for self-identification demands a personalised training plan.

MORE LINKED ATTACKS: COUNTERS

Some of the best war generals, e.g. Wellington, Napoleon, Genghis Khan, used the retreat and counter tactic with great effect. The same principle can be used in judo. The attacker attacks with two or three offensive moves, but allows an imperceptible weakness to creep into the developing movement. The opponent, sensing this growing weakness, counter-attacks the second or third one, which provides the opportunity the first attacker needs to counter the counter!

Here are a couple of examples. I have not provided much textual elaboration, but depend upon the action of the pictures. Study them closely and you will get a good idea how to do the counters.

Sequence 1

White attacks with sasai tsurikomiashi. Black steps over it and moves a couple of steps. White strikes again with ouchi. Black steps out. White stays where he is; he sees an opportunity for osoto and tries it. Black counters with osoto. (See photographs 38(a) —(i).)

38 **Combinations and counters**
(a) White is ready to attack: note the high hold of White's left hand — ready to pull Black's head down for the attack.

(b) White uses sasai and Black steps quickly over and moves away, making the pace fast.

(c) White reflects the pace and pursues Black for a couple of steps.

(d) White attacks with a fast ouchigari, but he does not get Black's head down.

(e) Black easily gets his right leg out of difficulties, and again moves away quickly.

(f) White, misjudging the pace (it's too quick), sees an opportunity for osoto.

(g) Black drops his right leg back ...

(h) and throws White with osoto for 10 points.

(i)

Sequence 2
Black attacks with a taiotoshi. White stumbles but immediately tries to stand up. Black attacks with uchimata on the bent knee. White rolls down. Black jumps on him, trying for a pin. White counters, also for a pin. (See photographs 39(a)—(i).)

39 Combination and countering
(a) Black is ready to attack.

(b) Black's taiotoshi knocks White down ...

(c) onto his left knee.

(d) Black attacks White's raised right knee with uchimata.

(e) White lands on his left side, for a small score; Black goes for 10.

(f) White uses Black's movement to roll him over.

(g) Black now has a problem!

(h) White moves into the attack.

(i) White moves up to Black's head (as he always should do if there is a choice).

(j) White clamps on a top-pin and wipes out Black's score by getting a full score of 10.

Back at the Contest

Things are slowing down. Both men are in the last phase of a numbing fatigue. They know they have to keep standing, but neither is quite sure how. Both have tried all they know, or perhaps we should say all they can remember. Red and White Sash cast a surreptitious peep at the clock. Good, only a few more seconds left. If only they can avoid making a stupid mistake from now on. Each man thinks he has a chance to win. What does Article 20 say?

'The referee will award the contest as follows:

(i) Where one contestant has scored ippon or equivalent, he shall be declared the winner.

(ii) Where there has been no score of ippon or equivalent, the winner shall be declared on the basis of: one waza-ari prevails over any number of yuko, one yuko prevails over any number of koka.

(iii) Where the recorded scores indicate no scores or are exactly the same under each of the headings (waza-ari, yuko, koka), the referee shall gesture and announce 'hantei.'

Before the announcement of 'hantei' the referee and judges must have assessed which contestant they consider to be the winner, taking into account the recognisable difference in the attitude during the contest or the skill and effectiveness of techniques.

The referee shall add his opinion to that indicated by the two judges and shall declare the result according to the majority of all three opinions.

Should the opinion of the two judges differ, the referee shall make the decision.

Where the referee has a differing opinion from that of the two judges after having announced 'hantei', he may delay giving his decision in order to discuss with them their reasons and thereafter once again announce 'hantei' and this time must give his decision based upon the

majority of three.

Once the referee has announced the result of the contest to the contestants it will not be possible for the referee to change this decision after he has left the contest area.

Should the referee award the contest to the wrong contestant in error, the two judges must ensure that he changes this erroneous decision before he leaves the contest area.

(iv) The decision of hiki-wake (draw) shall be given when there is no positive score and where it is impossible to judge the superiority of either contestant in accordance

with this article, within the time allotted for the contest.'

Red Sash thinks if he makes a last flurry of attacks (which he knows will have no chance of succeeding) he may be able to convince the referee he is the 'better man'. There is, of course, the risk of a counter, but not if he's very careful. He steels his body for one last effort; he throws himself at White Sash. In the hurly burly he hears the referee shout 'Sore made!' It's all over! Thank goodness for that! He breaks away from White Sash and both go back to their original positions.

The referee calls 'Hantei!' and momentarily waits ...

40 Group judo
Working together; thinking together.

INDEX

aesthetics 10, 60
arts 68
artists 61
attacks 22
    inside/outside 78

body-mind 68
body-weight 45
boredom 88
breakouts 20, 21, 22

camera 61
champion 10
chest contact 40
children 27, 28
combination attacks 60, 82, 87, 90
competition 29
co-operation 18, 29
coach 10, 28, 65, 66, 80, 82, 86, 88, 89
coaching 11, 16, 18, 21, 58, 59, 60, 66,
    71, 80, 88, 90
counters 60, 66

defence 22
discussion period 66
do-without-doing 51, 54

ethic 86
existentialism 89

feedback 16
feet 72
flexibility 11, 70
force 80, 82

grips 22, 23
groundwork 18, 27, 28, 29, 32, 33, 36,
    50, 54, 55, 66

habit 66
harmony 69
honour 10

injury 70

ju and go 80, 81

kata 11, 81, 86
kake 14, 18, 23
Kano 81, 86
kit 53

learning 28
lesson-plan 27, 28, 29
locks, arm 32, 33, 56, 57

mind 68, 69, 71
momentum 20, 21, 22
morals 10, 86
motivation, extrinsic and intrinsic 88
movement 11, 15, 17, 18, 27, 31, 60, 61,
    65
mysticism 68

objectives, of training 11
orient 88

parents 10, 28
personality 11, 86, 87
philosophy 80
Picasso 88
pins 18, 20
poetry 88
principles 26, 27, 31, 33
psychology 11, 87, 88

records 87
responses 11

Sartre 89
science 68
scores/scoring 8, 11, 14, 15
self-identification 89
shape 40

skills 10, 15, 18, 20, 22, 23, 27, 28, 29,
    31, 33, 35, 51, 60, 66, 68, 80, 86, 87,
    89
space 12, 13, 14, 17, 21, 23, 30, 40
speed 40
spin-turn 78
squads 87
strangles 32, 33
strategy 11, 56, 57

tactics 11, 53, 54, 58, 59, 73, 78, 87
talent 10, 89
technique 10, 11, 12, 13, 15, 18, 20, 21,
    23, 25, 27, 31, 33, 35, 58, 59, 60, 72,
    86
thinking 62
threat 78
throws 12, 15, 23
tiredness 71, 72
training 11, 22, 31, 59, 63, 68, 71, 72,
    80, 86
trial and error 16
turning, to attack 37

warm-down 29
warm-up 28, 65
waza 10